The Dark Side of Self-Publishing

A Brutally Honest Tell-All for Aspiring Authors

The Dark Side of Self-Publishing

A Brutally Honest Tell-All for Aspiring Authors

ISBN: 978-1-956581-59-1

ERIN GO BRAGH *Publishing*
Canyon Lake, Texas
www.ErinGoBraghPublishing.com

Contents

Introduction

The Dark Side of Publishing began as a section in my *How to Write, Market and Sell Children's Books* book. It was written to inform, warn and yet, inspire future writers and authors to follow their dreams, yet be aware that not everyone offering help is your friend.

This section of the book proved to be the most popular for numerous reasons. So, when I was asked to embellish upon it and maybe even create an eBook of just this content, I considered it. At first, I thought that it would be better to make sure people had everything they needed in one book, but then it was brought to my attention that not every author was going to pick up a *how to* for children's books even though this information was helpful for ALL authors of any genre.

So, since I was pulling aside this section, and formatting it for eBook, I decided to throw in some additional content not found in my previous *"How To Book"* as the additional content is relevant for all self-publishing authors to know and learn. Plus, enough time has passed that new scams and problems have arisen. Heck, if I sit on this six more months, I can likely add ten more pages – but how many people will be scammed in that time?

The world of books is ever evolving
and the writer who doesn't evolve with it
will go extinct.

While this is not a *know-all*, that covers every scam and issue out there, as there are new problems presenting themselves every single day, it should hopefully enlighten you and tip you on what to look out for. This book also focuses on the self-published route which also includes hybrid and vanity publishers as they all get categorized together. I did not dip my toe into the traditionally published authors problems because while they are plentiful, it just wasn't put on my heart to go into. Write what you know, and what I know better than anything else, is the self-publishing industry. Afterall, I am an author with more than 40 published books and I am a hybrid publisher for many great other authors as well.

My hope is always to educate and inspire.

Yes, the book publishing world can be dark and full of pitfalls, but if this is your God-given talent and you are following a dream, you should proceed with all of your heart and never give up. Just look before you leap!

The dark side of book publishing is just that, it is dark, it is mean, it is cruel and it can be just plain evil at times.

You walk into the world of writing with a song in your heart, flowers blooming, birds singing, a trickling stream in the background... You have a story idea that you want to share. You have a character that you're dying to introduce to the whole wide world. You have a dream that you want to see come true, and the book world is lining up to kick you until you go down, and then it will keep kicking you to keep you down.

That is not an exaggeration.

However, this book is not meant to be a deterrent but instead a warning. By wading into the writer's world, you are standing on the catalyst of something huge. You could become a smashing success! It *could* happen. You could be in the right place at the right time. You could write the next great novel. You could land the most amazing agent and publishing book deal. I'm not trying to dissuade you from trying. What I do want to do, is prepare you for what could happen if you are not that lucky. If you choose to go at it alone. Or if you step into this world without being fully prepared for the goods and the bads of this industry.

I work hard to push away pessimist feelings. I've been in this industry long enough, to know that, if I knew then, what I know now, and I didn't have that writer's gene forcing me to type out stories, I probably would have chosen another "hobby" a long time ago.

Other people instead think this will be fun and easy. They've watched those explainer videos touting how even a crappy book can sell millions; write it, heck, have AI write it, self-publish it and watch the Benjamin's flow in. They have been lying to you for years. That being said, I have been writing long enough to know that there's nothing else I want to do with my God-given talent.

A pessimist would tell you not to even bother trying. An optimist would go into all of this blindly thinking everything will simply work out. A realist would tell you to educate yourself and be prepared for all contingencies. My goal with this book is to take the pessimism of most authors who have already been in this industry long enough to know better, the optimism of newbie authors ready to dive into the deep end and mix them together to create realism.

If you tiptoe into this book business with a level head, knowing what could happen, and being prepared for what likely *will* happen, you will have a better chance at success. When you walk in expecting fireworks, and instead have a Molotov cocktail thrown at you, you tend to get a feeling of being burned. But when you walk in knowing that your life will be enlightened; your perspective on upcoming events will help you make better choices.

When I started writing this book, I did not think it would be very long. Some of these things have happened to me personally. Some of them have happened to authors that I know. Some of them were just stories that I read about in newsletters or on social media. The point is, if you are out there, they will find you, and it will likely happen to you. Be smart! Be prepared! And be ready to get into the dark side of publishing. This is not for the faint of heart.

There is an old saying if it was easy, everyone would do it. And yes, Amazon, Ingram, Draft 2 Digital, Lulu and a bunch of other self-publishing platforms have definitely made it easy to publish a book. That being said, publishing a book and selling a book are two entirely different things!

All of these platforms know that after you have spent the time to research and write a book, have it edited, get it formatted, either create a book cover or hire somebody to create a book cover for you, pay for illustrations, register the copyright, buy an ISBN number, and go through all the effort of publishing a book, you are not going to let your book sit stagnant without getting any sales.

These platforms and marketers know, that you are going to do everything you can to promote your book, including possibly, paying them for advertisement. That is, if you can afford to do so after forking out all of that money to create the book in the first place.

A decade plus ago, when self-publishing wasn't as prevalent, if you had a book in your hands, that meant you are an author.

To bookstores, libraries and schools they thought that meant that your story had been vetted, approved by a traditional publisher and gone through all the steps to make sure that your book met every criterion and was worthy of their consumers to purchase and read.

However, when self-publishing started to really take off, all of the previous rules of the book selling world, started to change – and not for the better.

Consumers hadn't realized yet that these books had not been properly vetted. That many of these books were not professionally edited, that the content may or may not have been proper for the demographic or the age group they were made for. They still opened up their doors and their bookshelves for you, but as with everything, there are those who have taken advantage of it, and in turn, ruined it for others.

I remember about 8 years ago being inundated by videos of people who claim that all you have to do is write a quick book and publish it to make millions. It didn't even have to be a great story, once it was published you would make millions. And so, people started doing just that. They were writing about things that probably should not have been written about, *but who am I to critique that?* They were putting out content that wasn't edited, large text on small pages for a 200-page novel that they charged $20 for it.

And now, with AI becoming prevalent, writing a book is super easy since AI can do it for you. AI can also do the illustrations for you. And for the average consumer who has not become wise to the situation, AI illustrations look great from a quick glance. The stories also sound great with a quick read. But they're not. They lack human emotion and connection. They are repetitive and bland. And as soon as consumers realize the difference between AI stories and AI illustrations, versus human stories and illustrations there will be even more discrimination to contend with.

A decade ago, libraries were happy for small self-published authors to come in and do readings and book signings, and set up a table and sell their book.

Nowadays, they don't want to have anything to do with it. And I'll tell you why. It's because of the backlash that they have received from their readers and consumers in regards to the content of the books that they put on their shelves.

While I am sure everybody who writes and publishes a book stands behind it, and they aren't just trying to make a quick buck. Likely those who are reading this book probably fall into that category.

There are plenty of people out there who write X-rated, pornographic, sexual crimes and torture, gay and lesbian material, without being up front about the content. To each their own I say, but graphic ratings should be included. Additionally, some of that content sometimes ends up in children's books and that should not be allowed. Period! While I am neither pro nor against book censorship, there is a time and place for everything. And there should be disclaimers if your content goes against the norm of society. But that is just me. Let the children keep their innocence.

So now, libraries don't want to allow self-published authors to sell their books and do readings and book signings at their facilities. They either say "no" altogether, so that way they aren't discriminating against the ones who are writing the material that they specifically don't appreciate, or they do a one-day event where all authors can show up and the consumers can decide what they want. This option is nice, but a lot of them have decided to stop doing that as well because of the cost involved.

I don't blame them there. In fact, a decade ago a small author would go broke trying to give a free book to every library because they only wanted donations. Nowadays, they don't even want the donations.

Because that means somebody has to spend the time to read the book and find out if it's worthy enough to put on their bookshelf, first.

They can't trust the author anymore because of the bad seeds who put out junk. It is really, really sad.

The new catch 22 is you have to prove that your book is worthy, have a ton of great reviews, show an excess number of sales, and have something that is being requested, before a library or bookstore will accept it.

But how do you do that if you cannot promote your book locally at your library, bookstores or schools?

That's the catch. *If it were easy everyone would do it.*

And now, because everybody is doing it, they've had to make it even harder to succeed. So, let's get into some of this and see how we can work with it.

Vanity Publisher Pitfalls

If you decide to go the self-publishing route, no matter which way you choose, the more you know the better you will be able to make informed decisions about the fate of your book.

When you publish a book, or have a book published, depending on your mindset, the very first thing that you need to make sure you know the difference about is the difference between self-publishing, hybrid publishing or vanity press publishing.

There is definitely a difference!

The self-publishing mindset is technically for anybody who chooses to put their book out there without going through a traditional publisher. Now there is a lot of confusion as to whether a company that decides to publish your book is a traditional publisher, hybrid publisher or a vanity press. So let's get a quick refence.

Traditional publishers and self-publishing companies both provide contracts. They both look through manuscripts, they both will get your book available to the market. But there is a huge difference!

Traditional publishers are going to vet your book. They're going to make sure that it meets all of their guidelines. That it is professionally edited. And then they will edit it themselves. That it is written for the market or they will make it so. That it is going to sell. And that it is going to sell a lot!

They provide a contract and they pay you in advance. That advance is not a, "here, we are paying you for a job well done" – it is a "here we are buying the rights to your book." You get paid to publish your book. But that advance is their buy out. It is important to know this fact because it is what sets them apart.

But this section is for those who are looking to self-publish, and who do not quite understand the difference between self-publishing, small press publishers, hybrid publishers, or vanity presses.

These *other* 'publishers' will read your submission, and if they so choose, will offer to publish your book, **for a cost.** And there is an awful lot involved in that cost. When you hear an author say "paying to publish your book" is a scam, they are right when discussing a traditional publisher. But they do not know the ins and outs of the self-publishing world. And if they do – they have such a low perspective of it, they think the whole thing is a racquet. They are wrong.

Many costs include: Professionally edit the book. Pay for illustrations. Paying for someone's time to do the formatting, book cover creation, as well as the time involved in publishing. Are they offering to market it? Create a book trailer video? Write a press release and distribute it? There's a lot to it. This is why they charge you for their services. But one of the most important things that I wanted to feature in this section are the pitfalls specifically from vanity publishers. Because they truly are the worst!

Vanity Publishers: Publish Everyone!

Vanity publishers are all about quantity, not quality. They don't critique your book, nor do they offer editing unless you pay extra for it. They'll tell you your story is "amazing!" which, while flattering, doesn't necessarily mean it's ready for publication. Not every manuscript is polished enough to be published, but vanity publishers don't bother reading your manuscript. Instead, they'll skim the blurb or summary you provided and, based on that alone, make an offer. They won't invest time into evaluating the full work. They just want your money.

One clear sign that you've encountered a vanity publisher is when you submit a manuscript that hasn't been professionally edited, and they claim it's "ready to publish." Unless you're a professional editor or a grammar expert, your manuscript likely needs revision. If you haven't paid for editing services or sought feedback from a critique group, you're doing a disservice to your book and yourself as an author. A first draft is rarely perfect, and no serious publisher would suggest otherwise.

If you can't handle critique or rejection, or if you think your first draft is flawless, writing may not be the right path for you. And if a publisher tells you your manuscript is ready for release without any editing or critique, it's a strong sign they're a vanity publisher.

Another red flag is when a publisher approaches you shortly after you've registered your copyright, without you ever submitting the manuscript to them. Legitimate publishers don't work that way—they wait for a submission, not a post-copyright registration.

Additionally, beware of publishers who contact you through social media comments or private messages. Traditional publishers do not use these informal channels to reach out to potential authors. If a publisher contacts you in this way, it's a clear indicator that they're likely a vanity press or scammer.

Vanity Publishers: Excessive fees, subpar services.

Vanity publishers often charge exorbitant fees for services that small presses or even freelance professionals can provide for far less. If a publisher asks you to pay $5,000 to $10,000 just to publish your book, run—*fast*. This is a clear sign you've encountered a vanity publisher.

Why do they charge so much? Because they know your book is your 'baby' and you will do anything for it. They also feel it is unlikely to sell well, and therefore, they can't rely on back-end profits from royalties. Why would they think that? Unless you have millions of followers or are a famous personality or celebrity, you likely won't be able to sell enough books to make millions. Instead, they make their money upfront, by charging authors high fees to publish.

One of the most egregious practices of vanity publishers is inflating the cost of printing. Often, they charge up to three times (or more) the actual cost of printing your inventory. Here's the thing: until your book is complete—meaning the final page count, formatting, and interior design are locked in—nobody can say exactly how much it will cost to print. But once those details are finalized, you should receive a clear printing cost and a retail price for your book, which, while typically higher than what traditional publishers charge, should still be reasonable and competitive for the market.

For example, if you're publishing a 300-page black-and-white paperback and it costs more than $5 or $6 to print, you're likely being scammed. This is one of the biggest tricks they pull.

I learned this the hard way. My first book was with a vanity publisher was a 200-page black-and-white paperback that cost me more than $10 to print. When you factor in shipping costs, royalties, and distribution fees, the book, which should have retailed for no more than $10, was priced at over $20.

No one is going to pay $20 for a thin, unknown author's book, especially when the cost of production was so high. The reason vanity publishers inflate these costs is simple: they know your book won't sell, so they make their profit off your inventory. They sell you your own inventory at overblown prices, keeping their hands in your pocket long after the book is published. They're like mosquitoes draining your resources.

They produce subpar books as well. Their cover creators are flipping designs so fast, they don't care if it meets market expectations, just that the author likes it. Their interior text flow is boring, plain and not artistic. They don't care if it's a beautiful book, just that it fits printer margins.

They use the same publishing platform as other hybrids, or self-publishers, so it's not like they have their own print facilities. And after your book has been published, good luck getting someone on the phone.

And their marketing services are the worst. I paid for a press release to be written and distributed. Not only was the release not news-worthy, (I am an author, I could have written it myself) it went out to a list of media that had changed their fax numbers due to spamming. Yes, I said Fax, it was that long ago.

They may offer you a website, but it is cookie-cutter and mimics every other author website they've designed – they are using a template.

Their print media, like the bookmarks and banners, consist of your book cover and author photo, but that is not what you want, *per se*, especially if you are writing a series or plan on doing additional books.

My list could go on; however, I would like to finalize this with an up note. If you're going to self-publish, and you are not going to ask for any help with any other services for your book, then this should cost you $0. If you are going to need help, but don't know where to start, then a small press or hybrid publisher would be a good fit. Let me explain.

Small Press or Hybrid Publishers charge for services.

Do you want a professionally designed book cover and you are not a graphic designer? Hire someone to do that. If you do not want to learn from the ample YouTube videos and newsletter tutorials on the internet how to format the interior of your book, then hire a text flow designer. Need illustrations and can't draw, hire an illustrator. This list can go on.

Those are all out of pocket expenses one must incur if you want something that looks professional. There are editors, purchasing an ISBN number, copyrighting your work... you can do all of this yourself or you can find a hybrid or small-press publisher that can do it for you. The point is, there are costs involved, but they should not add up to multiple thousands.

If they do and they cannot give you a breakdown of costs, they are likely vanity. Either that, or they are padding that cost for their own benefit and not yours.

Discrimination

Discrimination of the non-traditionally published.

A Letter to Share with Others:

We had an idea, a dream, a need to fulfill, a story to tell and we wrote it. We spent months, or years laboring over it until completion. We spent years and tears seeking representation, attempting to go the traditional route only to be met with closed doors and rejection. We went to critique groups, paid for editors, refused to give up and decided to become entrepreneurs in our already busy lives, taking on a second or even third job by self-publishing our book.

We paid hundreds, probably thousands of dollars on editors, illustrations, interior formatters, book cover creation, ISBN numbers, and printers, only to find once the book was in our hands ready to be presented to the world, that the work was only JUST about to begin. We spent time and money on exposure, marketing, advertisements, seeking reviewers, and writing press releases.

We contacted schools, libraries, bookstores and festivals. We bought pop-up tents, tables, chairs, book racks, banners, bookmarks and flyers. We spent our weeknights planning and preparing and our weekends doing events for the public.

Kathleen J. Shields

We kept a smile on our face as we watched our potential readers walk by without looking and we kept doing it because we knew someone would love our stories. We somehow did well enough to want to go through all of this again and write another book.

Each five-star review and sale only told us we were good enough. We discovered the price of admission for the American Library Association show, the large national book festivals and the closed doors of public schools and yet we did not let that deter us.

We are self-published authors. A league of our own. The little guy working against the machine that does all it can to belittle us, put up roadblocks and deter us. So, when you see one of us in your community, please don't look down on us like the traditional publishers.

We have heart. We have soul and we have drive. We just want to talk. We just want to inspire, and yes, we'd love to make a sale. But we know not everyone reads our genre, heck, not everyone reads! But every one of you are important to us. Each of you might have a friend who reads.

You could be a hero without spending a dime. You could help spread the word about our book. You could share our post or comment. You could help open the doors to those groups that have chosen to discriminate against us by overcharging for a booth, or not even allowing us access to their events.

You could let them know you would like to have options, choices and variety in your local bookstores, festivals, library meet and greets and school visits.

You want your youth to know that anything is possible in life, even writing a book. And you want equal opportunity for all. If you agree with this message, then, please feel free to share it!

Signed,

The non-traditionally published authors of the world.

Rejection

E ven if you choose not to attempt a traditional publishing contract, you will still receive rejection. Rejection comes in all forms. It's not just rejection letters from publishers and agents, it's not being taken seriously by the press, by high-end contests, by liberal arts organizations, sometimes even, by your public library, and parents as well.

There was a pop-up market in a nearby community where I live. I thought my books would do very well there. And they probably would have. However, I was not handmade or art. I pointed out that the illustrations were hand drawn and hand-painted by local artisans. That the text was handwritten by me. That literary art is still art. But they refused to let me in.

I've had parents walk up to me and see my educational series and ask, "are you a teacher?" "No, I'm not." To which they'd propose, "so you're a parent?" "No, I'm not." Then I'd get this look like "well then how do you qualify to write an educational book for children?"

Personally, I wanted to answer, how did you qualify to become a parent? But, no. I'd smile and explain that God put it on my heart, or I was once a child, or even, I have a life's worth of insight that I want to impart. Maybe you could mention that not every teacher starts their life as a teacher and not every preacher knew they were going to be a preacher.

I've seen large book festivals reject and/or discriminate against the self-published author. Oh sure, they allow them to submit their book, but they also require an extensive marketing plan to be submitted with it. They want to see its ranking. I don't blame them, but it makes it hard when the sales would in turn come from the event that you can't get into.

And one last story of rejection, and a little discrimination as well, a local library festival. A few years ago, they invited local authors to attend for free. That was so wonderful and generous. The next year they realized they didn't have room under the large event tents they rented so they said self-published authors would need to provide their own tents.

The next year, they had us pay for those spots and then this year, they said no self-pubs allowed. Really?

With the money you raked in from all of us hard-working authors just trying to gain exposure for our books, you didn't want us there, paying to be included? Guess you don't need financial donations for your library. What was the real reason?

Did we take too much focus from your precious traditionally published authors? The ones who can't be expected to setup tents, bring their own water or stand outside for too long?

Did you lose too many sales from the organizations with expensive memberships that were there showing their author's books but expecting the buyer to scan a QR code and purchase it from Amazon?

Do they not realize that people want to meet the author? That they want to buy a book and get it autographed? That they want to walk away with a product in their hand? Guess we just think too far out-of-the-box for them.

In recent years local libraries went from hosting new authors at their library for nice meet and greets and sales, to charging them all to be there for one day a year, together, to now not having anything at all for them. And don't even get me started on the donated books they received from us that they add to the giant 'Fill a bag for a quarter' annual book sales they have to support their Friends of the Library support groups.

Seriously, have you ever donated a book to a library and then visited a few years later to see if your book was still there? Did you donate a free book to be sold for a quarter or thrown away? I don't think so!

———————— ≫⟨◦⟩ ————————

Your Book is NOT for Everyone

I remember my first young adult book, I was certain everyone would love it. But really, I'm pretty sure grandparents wouldn't have gotten into it and it was not age appropriate for anyone under the age of 15. So, I was wrong in that mindset.

My Christian trilogy – I wrote it for young readers like 8-12, but YA and even adults get a lot out of it. Plus, it being Christian in nature, even grandparents could get a kick out of it. I was sure everyone would love it, but not everyone wants to read inspirational stories that symbolically connect to Jesus' life and the bible.

You always have to remember that no matter what, even if your book is completely amazing, incredibly well-written, professionally edited, a topic that almost everybody surely loves, highly marketed, receiving of five stars across the board, you're still not going to please everyone. And there will be one-star reviews.

One of my most popular books is "Hamilton Troll meets Dinosaurs." Everybody loves dinosaurs, or so I thought. Children *and* adults. When I was taught about dinosaurs in school, I was informed they existed millions of years ago. My mother was so excited, she brought out a pamphlet, 'The Sinclair Dinoland booklet' that she received from the World's Fair in New York circa 1964! I don't recall the details but the light in her eyes was brilliant!

When I was in school, I believe there were only like five types of dinosaurs. The Stegosaurus, the Brontosaurus, the Tyrannosaurus Rex, the Triceratops, and the Pterodactyl. Of course, nowadays, since Jurassic Park, scientists have been developing eras for each dinosaur. There are hundreds of breeds throughout the ages. I mean, the Raptor didn't exist in the 1970s. Not that I know of.

Anyways, not to get off topic, but the scientific information is always changing. What I was originally taught was "millions of years ago". But that information makes me a dinosaur as well, apparently.

Anyways, my book is for children. It is a rhyming, educational book of my character, Hamilton Troll who has a dream about meeting dinosaurs after visiting a dinosaur museum. It educates children about fossils, carnivores and herbivores but doesn't mention the names of each type of dinosaur. It also never specifies a timeline of dinosaurs in the story. The reason I mention this is because on the back blurb, and nowhere else, I wrote in the first sentence 'dinosaurs existed millions of years ago.'

Seems pretty harmless right? Nope!

I went to a very religious homeschool trade show. I was so excited! The series was perfect for them. I had created a homeschool curriculum book with language arts, math, and science. A book that was requested by the homeschool moms of a local town and of which I was assisted in. I was expecting it to be well received and I was expecting, as an author, to be swooned over. I really thought I would be sold out by the end of the weekend. And it was an expensive show to be at. Very expensive for me as I was only a couple years in to this venture and I didn't not have a lot of extra money to be throwing away.

Anyway, I had absolutely no idea that this particular group of homeschool parents believed that dinosaurs did not exist millions of years ago. They believe that dinosaurs existed a couple thousand years ago, in biblical times. While learning this was quite intriguing, and got my gears grinding out of curiosity, the way I learned about it was not so fun.

I had a woman walk into my booth, pick up my book, read the first sentence on the back blurb, and then proceed to yell at me at the top of her lungs because I wrote 'millions of years ago.'

She attracted the attention of every nearby booth vendor and passerby in the vicinity. She berated me in front of everybody and she was downright wicked about it. I was smiling while holding back tears. I didn't know what to do. I knew if I got angry back at her or tried to put her in her place that would not be professional or proper etiquette for a vendor or children's book author, so I thanked her for her information and asked her to explain more, to teach me.

I tried so hard to be kind to her even though she had single-handedly ruined my entire weekend. I think I sold maybe two books, one to each booth next to me, as pity sales. They tried to make me feel better but the embarrassment, the absolute disdain, ate me up.

All I wanted to do was tear down and go home Saturday evening, and instead, I returned Sunday morning as per my contract and stood there, almost in shame for another 8 hours. It was one of the most horrible experiences of my life, of being an author.

It will not define me though. 99.4% of the rest of the population in that age bracket love the book.

The point is, you cannot please everybody, but, you should try to do more research in regards to your topic to know why some people may not accept it and be prepared for possible kickback.

In a world of book banning, hurt feelings, and snowflakes being offended, you have to be stronger, braver, and smarter.

Friends Don't Share – Fans Do

T he most painful realization is learning that your friends and family don't really support your writing career. The truth of it is, they may buy the first book, or expect a freebie, but there's a slim chance they will read it. Maybe they DO read it, will they review it? Share it on social media? But will they be on board for the next books?

The average person's first book gets somewhere around 50 to 100 book sales initially. That is because you have cultivated your friendships, told your family, informed your co-workers, let your church friends know about the project, and you told them about it every step of the way. They know about it. They are ready to purchase the book. And one book purchase is pretty easy and affordable for most. But after the first month, when your first royalty report shows up, you realize there were very few, if any, online sales.

By the second month, you start wondering why there aren't any online sales. You sold so many books initially; *this is the way it was supposed to be every month*. At the very least, you expected all of your friends, family and co-workers to share your story with others, right? Unfortunately, the longer you are in the game the more you realize who your true friends are. And you can't even call them that. Because in the world of writing, they are supposed to be fans. And not everybody is going to be a fan of your work.

They may be your friend, but they are not going to be your fan. It is hard to differentiate between the two, especially when you are so close to somebody. You expect that friend to help you with your marketing efforts. You expect them to share the links on social media, write the reviews, help spread the word, but it is not in the friendship job description. It is not their duty as your friend, or family member. If they're not a fan, it is not their business.

Oh yes, they may say it's a good story, they may even say it's a great story, but is it really? They don't want to be the one who hurts your feelings. They want to be the friend who encourages you to keep following your dreams. Unfortunately, you cannot take what they say to heart. Also, they haven't read the books, newsletters, blogs and social media posts in regards to properly marketing your book.

They don't know all of the different steps that you, as the author, need to take to help get your book in front of the masses. If you ask them to do those things, you need to be very specific as to what it is that they need to do. Help make their job easier if they are going to share your information on social media. Provide them with pictures, and notes, and hashtags and links. Don't expect them to be able to figure all of this out on their own, because they won't. They are living very busy lives just like you are.

The worst thing that you can do as an author, is to have unspoken expectations of your friends that when they fail to follow through on, you get upset at them for. That is not fair.

No matter how much it hurts you, that they didn't take the initiative, time or effort to read your book, leave a review, or share your post, it is not their job to do that. Don't forget that.

They assume that your book will do well on its own. That the proper audience for its genre will find the book and do all of that for you. There are even some who may feel that if they push your book for you, they are biased based on the fact that you are friends. And sadly, there are others who have no intention on reading your book and therefor will not share or push your book for fear that it may include something they would disagree with.

Review Hurdles

Getting people to leave reviews for books is like pulling teeth from a very awake feral cat, it could be downright painful to you!

Say you try to get reviews before the book is published through advanced reader copies. You sign up for a promotion, have people sign up, send them a free eBook, and await a review. If you're lucky 5% of those people will actually leave a review when the book comes out. Lack of follow through is real.

So, you sign up for promotions to get the book out after the release. A ton of people sign up. A ton of people receive a free eBook. A very small fraction of them may leave a review, if any.

You do a big public book event, or Festival. Sell hundreds of books to adoring fans. It is likely none of them are going to think to go to Amazon and leave a review. Even if you ask them to leave a review, they're not going to remember. And most importantly, a lot of them don't know that they *can* leave a review for a product that they did not buy on Amazon. Granted, verified purchase reviews mean a lot more than just a generic review, but when you're first starting out, any review is better than no reviews at all.

Educating the public on reviews, following up on all of the free eBook promotions that you sent out, it's time-consuming. And frustrating.

Amazon removes friend & family reviews.

Amazon does not like it when friends and family leave reviews because they consider them biased. If they find out that friends and family are leaving reviews, they will likely remove them.

If any of your advanced readers mention that you gave them a free book in exchange for a review, Amazon will see it as a paid for review and remove it. Educating your reviewers is just as hard as getting reviews. And losing those hard-earned reviews is even more painful. It is all part of the game.

No Amazon account

It may be beyond your comprehension, as it is mine, but there are a lot of people still to this day do not use Amazon to purchase stuff. I know, it baffles the mind, but there are people who don't use Amazon. And so those people, even if they create an account for you to leave a review, unless they have spent $50 they can't leave a review. It used to be $50 in the lifetime of their account, now I have heard that it is $50 per calendar year. So, if you have readers who are willing to leave a review but do not have Amazon accounts, you can suggest that they leave it on Barnes & Noble, or Goodreads, or some other review website. They could even simply post it on their social media profile to share with their friends. Anything helps.

Children's Book Reviews

If you think regular reviews are hard to get, just try to get reviews for children's books! Think about the fact that most children's picture books are read to the child at bedtime. The mother is tired, the child is not, and many books have to be read before the child will pass out. Or, if the child loves the book, they ask for it to be read to them over and over again, and that again, exhausts the parent. Technically, by the time the child is asleep, the parent is ready for a glass of wine, or to pass out themselves.

However, in many cases, they still have dishes to do, clothes to wash, toys to pick up, and a house to straighten before bed. The last thing they are thinking about doing is logging into their Amazon account to leave a book review. And by the time morning comes around, there are way too many things to do to log into Amazon and leave a review.

The fact of the matter is, it is incredibly difficult to get a parent to leave a review. You know you can't get children to leave a review, so that leaves grandparents. They aren't good about that either. Even if they're technologically savvy enough to know that they should and that they can, they tend to buy the book for the grandchild and mail it to them. They have no idea whether the child actually liked the book or not. Or, they hold on to the book until the child comes to visit, once or twice a year? Are they going to remember to leave reviews? Doubtful.

Don't let the numbers deter you.

"My book looks like a failure online because there aren't any reviews." You may think that, and others might also, but the reality is that people don't think to leave reviews, especially for children's books. So don't let that deter you.

You're going to find that you will sell a lot more books face to -face than you will online, especially for children's books, so don't let the sales ranking numbers online bum you out. Just because your book isn't ranking online does not mean that it's sitting stagnant unless you are not able to go out to events and promote and sell your book.

Don't think that if you go to a large book festival with a hundred other authors, that you're a failure if you don't sell any books. You're literally competing with a hundred similar items (books) and a hundred similar people (authors). While every book is different, and the topics span the spectrum of interests, the average consumer, can only afford to buy a few books that day. I'm sure they would love to buy one book from each author, but that is unrealistic.

The good news is, that almost everybody has a child in their life. A child, grandchild, a student, a niece, or nephew. Children's books are easier to sell than adult books. Which is why doing public festivals is so successful.

When an author is trying to sell a romance, a historical memoir, a fantasy novel or other such genre, they are trying to find very specific people walking in a sea of people. They do better with online sales because those people, one, have their own money, and two, do their own shopping. They search for precisely what kind of books that they are looking for, and purchase what they want. Marketing to them is a lot easier.

But children's books online cannot sell themselves, because people cannot open them up and make sure that they are safe, clean reads. They don't have the author standing there telling them the quick elevator sales pitch of what the story is about. They can't be told in 5 seconds, the gist of the story and the lesson inside. Not like you can do when you are face-to-face.

When you're in public, and they walk up to you, and they look at your book, you can sell them in a few seconds, if they are interested. And that is precisely why you should never give up. Why you should not let the depression take over, and why you should not be deterred. You may think you can't do this. You may begin to think you aren't made for this. You may even begin to consider that you aren't a real author, that you are an imposter compared to the successful authors out there. **Don't!**

Contests – Should you?

Contest claims to help you sell a book if you win, but the sticker only does so much if people see the book with it on it. The win doesn't promote your book, but it does help you feel better about yourself, your writing and your skills.

Some contests will send out a press release, some do interviews, some share on their social media, all of this is good, but after a while, gets over-looked by the masses. There are ALA contests that if you win, really get recognition, posters for every school library to hang on the wall (ideal) but they are very difficult to win. Fortunately, all they cost is your time and a few books mailed to them.

Other contests can charge $100 up to $500 or more to enter. They are gambles. Do you feel lucky? Can you risk losing that money? It depends on how strongly you feel about your book. The question is to look at it – realistically. Everyone thinks their story or book is great – but compared to the traditionally published books, compared to previous years' winners, how does it stack up? What dets your book apart and makes it deserve the spotlight? If it's just a 'good story' but it's not the next great novel, think about this gamble, first.

Let's jump ahead to winning that contest, first place, second place, runner up – there is recognition and a sticker – as I mentioned before. That sticker, shiny, gold or silver will shimmer in the light and draw their eye to your book – if it is sitting one a shelf cover-out and not the spine. At a tradeshow, that draws in the customer. If it is seen online, yes, it gives it a bit more credibility, especially if they recognize the contest. But the catch with all of this is – they must see it.

The difficult part about promoting a contest win, shy of the social media or email blast to those customers who've likely already bought the book, is getting strangers to find it. That's where marketing and advertising come into place. The catch – if you market it in writers and authors groups, you are not marketing it to your readers and you are telling other authors that this is a winnable contest.

Besides, now there is a debate on whether you should put stickers on your books! There are authors who use the sticker "Autographed by the Author" or just "Autographed" like what Barnes & Noble does if you are successful in getting a book signing there and they order a few books for their shelves.

Personally, I like that sticker! It tells me how unique this book is compared to the same priced book on Amazon. Same with contest stickers. But some authors have stated they don't like the stickers to busy up their book cover or ruin it if it gets torn off. I get that – but the ultimate decision is yours of course My opinion is, anything that can help set you apart – DO!

Starving Artists

I remember when I was maybe **9 or 10** years old, being dragged to a hotel convention center with a generic banner outside stating 'Starving Artist Sale'. With my hand in my mother's hand, she dragged me into this room full of large canvas paintings. Hundreds of them were lined up against the wall, one leaning against another, in stacks many feet deep. There were more ships in the oceans, churches in a field of flowers, and longhorns standing in bluebonnets, than I had ever seen in one place. And almost all of these were very inexpensive to purchase (especially when you learn what it should cost!)

The term starving artist produced a vision in my head of an artist sacrificing a meal to buy paint, brushes, or a canvas so they can get the beautiful image in their head painted for the world to see. I did not know the cost of a canvas, of purchasing every color paint in the spectrum and all the specialty brushes of varying sizes, but even as a child I knew that at those prices, they're probably was not that much markup for them to pay their bills. I did not meet any of those starving artists, but I understood the term quite well.

The term, Starving Artist,
works very well for writers as well.

Artists, writers, musicians, we are all part of a very similar group of people. We are following a path set forth before us attempting to express our creative abilities and talents for the rest of the world to see, hear, read, and enjoy.

Just like the different art categories, like abstract, floral, sunsets, animals, and religious, writers work within various categories as well. Just like musicians specialize in either, rock, pop, jazz, Christian or instrumental, writers have their go-to genre as well. Each one of us artists have something unique and different to provide the world, and we do whatever we can to share it, no matter how difficult and how little financial benefit we see.

Writers do have it tough, but not as hard as artists. I mean at the very least, take into account wall space. Look around your house, how many blank walls do you have? How many walls don't have windows, doors, or furniture up against them? When somebody is looking for art, they're looking for their particular genre, a particular size, a particular color palette, and at a particular price. They are only going to buy one. At least with books, you can fit quite a few of them on a bookshelf. Selling a book is a lot easier than selling artwork, but it is not as easy as some may think.

You Don't Get Paid an Hourly Wage

I have a friend who makes jewelry. Beautiful jewelry. She casts the metal, sets the stones and builds the jewelry. Bronze, Copper and sterling silver. It is amazing stuff and people come back all of the time for a new piece. She was talking to me this last weekend about how many hours she puts in creating and manufacturing a necklace. She adds in the cost of the stones, and she figures out her wholesale cost along with her retail cost. She actually gets to earn an hourly wage on her products. Writing a book is not like that.

How many hours did you spend writing this book of yours? How many hours did you spend researching, and editing? How much money did you spend on illustrations, interior text flow and formatting, book cover design? How much does an average, book sell for retail? A quick online search pulls up the school library journal reports that children's books usually retail for between $6.49 and $17.85 per copy. Hard covers command the highest prices, with mass-marketing paperbacks getting the lowest price.

Trade paperbacks are somewhere in the middle. That means, your chapter book which is paperback black and white paper, shouldn't be more than $10 to $12. Your hardback full-color picture book should not retail for more than $19.95. If you were purchasing inventory, print on demand, to sell directly, you're paying somewhere between $3 and $5 for a chapter book, and $8 to $12 for a picture book. You take that off of what your set retail price would be, and that is how much money you have made per book.

So, when you add up all the time and hours you spent writing, editing, formatting, the money you spent purchasing illustrations, doing a book cover and marketing, that's how much you are worth. What does that come up to? Pennies per hour? I mean seriously!

Selling your books at a free table at a bookstore or a library is nice, but that's not where the people come to shop. If you do festivals where you pay to be a vendor, how many of those books do you have to sell to break even? I've done many shows where I didn't even pay for the show with the number of books that I sold. I've done some shows where I sold a lot of books, but by the time I took off what I paid to be there, I may have made 10 bucks. And it was hardly enough to cover the gas I spent to get there.

I did not cover my time and effort for being there, and completely forget about the number of hours I spent writing, developing my craft, and paying for the services needed to finalize my books.

This industry actually sucks if you want to make money in it. You cannot price your book what you feel your time is worth, otherwise your book would be $2,000 each. Yes, if you sell millions of books those pennies per book start to pay off, but unfortunately, the average self-published author sells about 200 books in its life time. I'm sure you'll sell more, but is it enough?

If you are jumping into the writing industry to make money, I highly suggest you rethink that. If you are here just to make money, do jewelry instead. You can earn more profit in one sold necklace than you would in 50 sold books. You will save your back from having to lift large boxes of heavy books as well.

If you are writing because that is what has been placed upon your heart to do, then you are doing it because of that and that fact alone. Not for the fame, not for the fortune, partly for the legacy, but because I wanted to give something meaningful to the world. Oh yes, fame and fortune would be nice, and is possible with hard work, luck, and a great product, but it doesn't happen easily, it does not happen overnight, and it is incredibly rare. This is one of the many things you should be aware of if you want to tiptoe into the writer's pool.

Do this for the LOVE of Writing & Nothing More.

The Depression is Real

Why isn't my book selling? I see it over and over again on social media and all of those writers' groups. Why don't I have tons of reviews? Why can't I make this work? I feel like I have tried everything and now I feel like a failure.

The depression is real. It comes to each of us. The mindset of becoming a New York Times best-selling author, with hordes of people lining up at every one of your book signings has been ingrained into our imaginations. We believe that if that isn't happening, if we aren't number one best-sellers, if we go months without selling a book, we're failures. But we are not. That couldn't be further from the truth.

"Don't let slow sales deter you from being an author. You might be a great writer but a horrible salesman."
Angel D.

You have to remember the stats. How many people are on this planet? How many people think about writing a book? How many people start the process? How many people actually finish writing the book? How many people go forth with the effort of editing, revising and seeking a publishing route? How many of them stop after the first or second or 10th rejection? How many of them actually decide to self-publish? How many of them start marketing their book? Get on social media and put themselves out there? How many of them do book festivals, fairs and craft shows?

When you get down to the stats, you'll find, that if you did each one of these steps, and if you are continuing to do these steps, then you are not a failure. If anything, you have succeeded where millions haven't even tried.

I repeat, You Are NOT A Failure!

Yes, the process can be quite daunting. The lack of sales, the lack of exposure, the lack of reviews, the lack of referrals, the lack of comments on social media, the lack of likes, can all get you down. But don't forget, you are a small cog attempting to fit in a big machine, a huge machine, that does not want you anywhere near it!

The traditional publishing companies do not want you to succeed, because that means they will fail. And trust me, they are starting to see the writing on the wall. They're pandering to small-minded political mindsets and old-school thought processes while utilizing all of the connections and funds they have accumulated to buy their placement in the world of book sales.

Read that again.

They buy their placement!

They buy their reviews. Does it really make sense that the make-or-break review is the Kirkus or the Clarion and it costs as much as $500 to get?

They buy their bookstore shelf space and their bestselling categories. They buy their New York times ad placements. Have you ever wondered how a book can become a best-seller before it's even released? Never thought about that... until now?

A traditional publisher sends out a mass notification to all of the bookstores, 600 Barnes & Noble bookstores, 260 Books-A-Million bookstores, and about 10,000 other bookstores. Of course, the number of bookstores has drastically dropped in the past decade, primarily due to Amazon but this is just an example.

Anyways, they say the next great book is coming, so the bookstores purchase a dozen for their bookshelves. *Pre-orders.* Yes. But that's already easily 120,000 books before the release date. So yes, they're touting best-seller before the book has even been released.

They're selling their inventory to bookstores across the nation. They're telling all those bookstores that this is going to be a best-seller, and the bookstores are buying it. Then they're telling all of the readers that this is a best-seller and so they run out to buy it when it is released. The average reader assumes it's an amazing story if it is a best-seller. That's the way it works, right? But no one besides the publisher has even read the book. Maybe a few reviewers, *but best seller?*

How many times have you picked up a traditionally published book and found spelling and grammatical errors? How many times have you finished a book and closed it and just felt nothing, or disappointment? It's not a bestseller, not the way you and I think it is.

Best-seller should mean that it is an amazing story and because it is such an amazing story, word got out and that caused it to become a best seller. Not the other way around. But in the big publishing world, it just means that all the bookstores purchased it. It doesn't even mean it's going to sell to you and me, the average consumer. And it might not! But by then it doesn't matter. By then, if in 6 weeks or 6 months, the bookstore hasn't sold the book, they just send it back to the publisher and the publisher will come up with something else to do with it. That is the way it works.

So it was a best seller to bookstores, but not the consumer. They bought that title of bestseller. We can't afford to do that. When you sell a book, when you sell many books, when you continue to sell your book at every event that you do, you are succeeding where they very likely could be failing. Remember that!

And when your books keep selling year after year, you will have succeeded where every other traditionally published author has failed. Remember, if they don't meet their sales quota by the end of the year, their book is done. The publishers bought the rights and will not spend any more of their money printing and marketing a failing book. And because they bought the rights to your book, you can't take it and self-publish it later.

Ghostwriters for popular author names.

Ghostwriters don't get any recognition. How many books have you read by a popular author, traditionally published, that was ghost written by somebody else? It happens more often than not. You can tell that it's not the same author. You can read it in the story, the way it is written. It doesn't sound like the author. Those traditional publishing companies are using small writers like us to write the stories and then using the names of popular authors to sell it. How can you possibly compete with that? You want your name to be the book that people talk about, not Michener, Grisham, Steel, King or Koontz.

Yes, ghostwriters make a very good amount of money, but the one thing they don't make is recognition. They don't get to take credit for the story they wrote. They don't get to tout it in their portfolio. They don't get to build the street cred to promote themselves to agents or other publishers. And to be honest why would a publisher take the chance on a book written by someone that nobody knows when the same story with King's name will literally fly off the shelves?

But I am a no-name author...

So was Orson Wells before he wrote *The War of the Worlds* and caused chaos across the nation. So was Jules Verne before *Twenty Thousand Leagues Under the Sea* helped people picture a working submarine.

Even DaVinci died thinking he was a complete failure when in fact, everything he sketched in his notebooks were "centuries ahead of their time!"

"When we write, we build not just worlds, but futures. When we sketch, create, and imagine, we lay the building blocks for others to try to reimagine our dreams and turn them into something tangible. Something that works."
~ *Author Angel Dunworth*

Do you think Gene Roddenberry knew that his communicators and tricorders in Star Trek were going to become today's cell phones and computers? That his food replicators are coming to life with 3D food printing. While we are still waiting for the Holodeck, we are close with virtual reality. And teleportation is coming... why do I say that? Because it was imagined!

If you can imagine it, you can bring it to life. It may take time, maybe more time than you have here on this earth, but it could happen. That is why you do this.

That is why you write. For the legacy! If you write and sell a book to a child, it leaves a lasting impression on their heart. They will keep it on their bookshelf, and pass it down to their children and their children's children. You may not make millions of dollars but you ARE making memories, leaving a legacy and inspiring the future - and that is worth something.

Imposter Syndrome

I've made it! I've got a book signing at Barnes & Noble. I've been accepted into a book festival with an assortment of other successful published authors. I've been invited to present my book to a school assembly... But I don't know if I deserve it. Am I a fraud? Sure, I wrote a book, but am I smart enough for the school assembly? Am I articulate enough to compete with all of those other successful authors? Does my book stack up to all the other books that qualify to be on a Barnes & Noble bookshelf? Am I an imposter?

What is impostor syndrome?

Imposter syndrome is a psychological pattern in which an individual doubts their skills talents or accomplishments and has a persistent and internalized fear of being exposed as a fraud. Despite all of the external evidence of their competence, and their success, they still have a nagging feeling that has convinced them that they do not deserve everything that they have achieved. Sometimes these people will attribute their success to either luck or timing. Maybe they think that they outsmarted somebody but that doesn't allow them to think that they are more intelligent than the other.

The fact of the matter is, who does qualify to be on a panel of authors? How can you compare yourself to a Harlequin romance author? How can you compete with historical fiction, or even historical accuracy in an educational textbook? How can you compete with a scientific or medical journal? Who are you compared to Stephen King, Danielle Steele, or James Michener? You are someone who followed through with an idea, completed a written story, edited it, illustrated it, published it, marketed it, and was found.

Who qualifies to present a new children's book to a dozen classes at school? Are you a teacher, or a professor? Do you have an educational degree? What qualifies you to present a brand-new story to elementary school-age children? What if you don't even have children? What makes you an expert? You are someone who followed through with an idea, completed a written story, edited it, illustrated it, published it, marketed it, and was found, no matter where, and sold a book.

Who does qualify to have their book for sale at a Barnes & Noble bookstore? You are not a big-name author. Your name is not a household name. You are not a musician actor/actress, movie star, influencer, or other worldly popular entertainer. You do not have a fan base of millions. You do not have radio, TV, and theater exposure to the masses. You are not even making thousands of sales per month. Why would a Barnes & Noble bookstore waste their precious, and expensive shelving space on a no-name author?

Because you are someone who followed through with an idea, completed a written story, edited it, published it, marketed it, and was found and accepted.

Who am I to write a "How to Write, Market and Sell a Children's Book" book? I am someone who has followed through with dozens of story ideas. I have completed more than 40 books of multiple genres. I have paid for editors, received hundreds of critiques, found ARC reviewers, and publicists, and done advertisements. I have received tons of five-star reviews, won awards and received recognition. I have been in the industry for more than 25 years. I have learned a ton of the ins and outs, and I have seen what works and what fails.

Am I a success? I guess that depends on your interpretation of success. If your idea of a success is somebody who can quit their day job, and just write books all day long and have millions of dollars in the bank account, you might need to readjust your thought process. It has not been that way for decades. Even traditional publishers who pay you an advance, expect you to spend that money on marketing.

Even if a traditional publisher asks you for a three-book deal, you still have to find the time to market the first book while writing the second and third. You still have a full-time job, and you still may not make it.

And if that first book doesn't sell the way they hoped, they can renege on your next two books.

Plus, as you have read in previous chapters, you have one year if you're lucky to make it, otherwise, you will be back to your old day job. In fact, your traditional publishing advance likely won't even allow you the financial opportunity to quit your day job.

To define success, I ask:

- Did I write my best story?
- Did I put my best work out there?
- Did I market it to the best of my abilities?
- Did I get good reviews?
- Did I put all the time & effort into it that I should?
- Am I happy with the job that I did?
- Am I willing to put in the same effort for the next book?
- Am I willing to keep advancing my experiences to better myself in the future?

THAT is what a success is!

Most people in this industry, or who want to break into this industry, have an idea. But they don't write it down. Or if they write it down, they don't embellish upon it. They never finish the story. If they do finish the story, maybe they don't pay for professional editing? Maybe they go the cheap route on a book cover. Maybe they hand-draw their own illustrations instead of hiring a professional illustrator? (Note, some authors DO have the talent for both.) Maybe they just published it on Amazon but didn't pay for advertising. Maybe they didn't create social media accounts, and try to market their book. Maybe they didn't send the emails, the letters, or make the phone calls to the schools, the libraries, the local bookstores, or sign up for the trade shows.

Maybe they did all of that and only sold 100 books. Does that make them a failure? No it does not!

Make note of how many times, as you are sitting there talking about your book, or trying to sell your book, that somebody else comes up to you and says "hey I have an idea that you should write about". Or, "I've been thinking about writing a book... how should I start?" Or, "I want to publish a book." How many of them do you think are going to follow through with that desire? Maybe you can encourage them.

You followed through. I know this because you picked up this book. Because you read it. You are willing to put forth the effort to learn everything that you can and will continue to learn as you go forth in this challenge.

You should know, that 80% of the population has the desire to write a book. But did you know that 97% of the people who start writing their books never finish them? If you do finish your book, you are already in the top 3%. That, in itself, is an accolade.

Mathematically, that works out to - out of every 1,000 people that set out to publish a book, only 30 complete the task. And then if you add on top of that the fact that only 20% of those people who wrote the book actually publish it, actually follow through and finish all of the details and self-publish. That means that out of a thousand people, only six people walk away with a book.

Many of the reasons they don't follow through, is they didn't have the money to have it professionally edited. Or maybe they didn't feel that the book was good enough. Maybe they're trying to be too perfect, procrastinating enough so that book will never see the light of day. Maybe they tried to get in with the traditional publishers and received enough rejections that they chose not to even proceed forward. Maybe they thought that the self-publishing route would be too difficult and time-consuming, or wouldn't pay off in the long run. *They might have been right...*

But then again, that makes them the imposters. If you have been invited to a bookstore for a book signing, to a school for a presentation, or to an author event, that means you are an expert in your field. You may not be the most popular author, the most successful author, or the most educated author, but you ARE an author. And you are the only one standing in that bookstore, or that school that is.

Take pride in the knowledge that you have followed through to see your dream become a reality. And then continue to better yourself every step of the way.

Amazon, the Devil You Know

A mazon can sometimes feel like a powerful force, offering opportunities that come with unexpected costs. For self-published authors, though, Amazon is a god, but are they good? This is not an anti-Amazon message, just a feeling I get... a lot.

Plus, how can I say that? This book in your hands was published on Amazon, and for many authors, it's the platform where most of their sales come from. But if you look at it from a different angle, if you look at it with a little creative imagination, you might start to see the complexity of the situation.

As a writer, what's your ultimate goal? To get your book into the world. But at what cost does that come?

What do you want, as a writer? To publish your book. Are you willing to sell your soul for it? No, of course not, but if you self-publish, you are going the easy route. Amazon is giving you an opportunity to become a star and they are offering it for free. Sure, sounds like that devil offering me a wish...

Now don't take that as my saying everyone who self-publishes sold their soul or that only traditionally published authors are stars, this is just a loose metaphor. My point is, if someone offered you a magic bean, would you plant it and see where it goes, or would you keep walking? My guess is, you'd be willing to plant it and let it grow. Especially if you didn't know it came at a cost. So, lets get into this.

The devil deceives.

The devil deceives because he wants to reel us in like a fish on a hook and make us his slaves. Powerful entities often have ways of drawing you in that aren't immediately obvious. Amazon's KDP self-publishing platform offers many benefits, but it's important to consider the full picture before deciding if it's the perfect opportunity for you.

If you self-publish with KDP and don't use your own ISBN number, it shows as independently published. Technically the owner of the ISBN number is the official publisher and if you use Amazon's free ISBN, they are your publisher. Sure, their terms and conditions say you are the publisher and retain all rights, but what happens to your content after you die?

If you don't have any heirs Amazon keeps it all. If you do have heirs, you will need to write it into your legal will and/or provide details and account access. They will need to present the will and the death certificate to have the items transferred into their account. If they don't have a will with your wishes, your heirs could be left without your legacy. And trust me, even that process is lengthy and difficult to accomplish.

The devil is a trickster.

Tricksters, after all, often create situations that challenge you to find creative solutions. This can be a positive thing, right? Creativity and imagination are key to an author's ultimate work.

However, a trickster who offers you an immediate win, like a free spin on a slot machine, might encourage you to keep playing, possibly spending more of your own resources in hopes of another win. By offering a free way to publish your book, Amazon makes money on the inventory you purchase, the sales you generate, the leads you create, and the advertisements you pay for to boost visibility.

Some powerful systems make things seem simpler than they really are. While Amazon provides an accessible route to publishing, they also benefit from the hard work authors put in—often in ways that may not be immediately clear. Their business model is built on facilitating your success, but it also ensures they profit significantly from that success, and sadly, even your failures.

The devil has dominion.

We all know Amazon is the biggest online marketplace in the world! But who is the biggest bookseller on the planet? While you might think of names like Barnes & Noble, Walmart or even Books-A-Million, Amazon is the undeniable leader.

The Kindle, their e-reading device, is dominant in the market today and has become synonymous with e-books. Much like how people refer to tissues as Kleenex, Amazon's name has become nearly interchangeable with online book shopping.

For Prime customers, the free shipping advantage makes it hard for other retailers to compete, especially when adding the cost of shipping to the price of a book. With other bookstores who offer free shipping on orders over a certain amount, they still can't compete because it is less cost-effective to buy through them, when you only need or want one book.

Additionally, if KDP is your sole printer and publishing platform, it can sometimes feel as though you are tied to them for the long haul, no matter how you feel about their terms or fees.

The devil plants doubts.

Many self-published authors start out with high hopes, only to find that their sales don't take off as expected. With the realization that marketing is key, they begin promoting their books on social media, running ads, and paying for visibility on Amazon.

However, the complexities of algorithms, high competition, and the rising costs of advertising can make it challenging for new authors to break through. When larger players are willing to spend more on ads, it can push smaller authors down in the rankings, making their efforts feel less effective.

Of course, some authors do find success and manage to master the marketing game—but for many writers, who would rather focus on writing their next book, the time and energy required to learn the intricacies of marketing can be overwhelming. This can lead to feelings of doubt, not about their writing, but about their ability to navigate the marketing side of things, which is not their primary passion.

Unfortunately, in today's market, success is often defined by sales, visibility, and the financial rewards that come with it.

The devil tempts with sexual immorality.

There are times when success in publishing can seem closely tied to content that appeals to more base instincts. Amazon offers a platform for authors to publish a wide variety of works, but that doesn't always mean that every type of content aligns with the values we want to share with the world.

For some authors, particularly those who write in genres like children's literature or Christian fiction, it can be disheartening to see certain types of content, often more explicit or sensational in nature, seem to dominate the sales charts. While it's important to recognize that every genre has its own audience and place in the market, the question arises: should an author compromise their morals for the sake of sales?

Personally, I believe that if I wouldn't feel comfortable sharing my work with my community or standing by it in any setting, then I have to reconsider whether it's the right choice for me. Writing and publishing should feel authentic. But at the same time, the pressures of commercial success can lead some authors to consider writing what sells, even if it's not aligned with their true calling. The key question becomes: ***How do we stay true to our values while still making a living and reaching readers?***

The devil will slander you.

As authors, we often face situations where external factors can affect our work in ways we can't control, even when we're doing everything right. When things go wrong, it can be the author who bears the brunt of the consequences, especially when mistakes are made in areas like production or shipping.

For instance, when an error happens that the author has no control over; like shipping delays, damaged products, or incorrect items being sent—the buyer may not always understand that the issue lies with the fulfillment process, not with the author. These mistakes can result in negative reviews that impact the book's reputation, as well as yours.

There are also occasional issues during the printing process itself. For example, books may have errors, or the color quality being off due to printer maintenance issues. Two books can accidentally be combined under one cover. Printers get jammed and pages are printed upside down, sideways or cockeyed. Paper isn't cut all the way through and you can't open the book. Too much glue was used on the cover and so pages are stuck together. Printer ran out of ink and so the color is off. The list can literally go on.

While these situations are frustrating and out of the author's hands, they can still negatively affect the reader's experience, leading to reviews that don't reflect the author's original intent or quality of work.

Two of my own personal examples:

One time there was a printer issue and the last 10 pages of a gay sex coloring book was printed in the front of my children's inspirational coloring book. I was fortunate to not receive a negative review and they just returned it, but that return, was then shipped to me to pay for, which is how I found out about the print error. How often does that happen and I never knew it? No, I didn't pay for it and instead got a credit – but again I ask, how often does something embarrassing like that happen?

Another one that I have experienced a number of times, is the fact that the 13-digit ISBN numbers that I (and you) pre-purchased years ago, are not how Amazon organizes their products. They convert a 13-digit ISBN number to a 10-digit number which in my case, was also being used by a Chinese company selling men's underwear.

You can imagine my shock when I go to check one of my educational children's book product pages and see men's underwear instead. And we're not talking about boxers. No, we are talking about very tight, shadows accentuated around the contents and a magnified size in order to sell their product. It was dang near pornographic, and it had my book title and name next to it. I've had to contact Amazon many times to have them fix it. Later on, it happened again, this time for my poetry book. Sometimes I wonder if it would have

The Dark Side of Self-Publishing

helped with sales… lol – I guess I'll never know. I was WAY too embarrassed to let that stand and I pray it doesn't happen again.

That being said, it would not surprise me. It is beyond my understanding why we buy a code that is 13 digits and Amazon converts it to 10. Especially with how many products they have on their site… but I don't make the rules or have anything to do with their lack of common sense.

Here's the screen capture of my poetry book – for those who were excited to see it. Haha!

A Rhyme for Everything: Rhythmic Poetry for Everyone Paperback – October 23, 2019
by Kathleen J. Shields (Author)
5.0 ★★★★★ ∨ | See all forms

There's an ocean of emotion when it comes to writing rhyme. It takes a bit of patience to flow each word in time is important, the bounce and flow is most. You never know what feelings will wash up on the coast. This book ha levels: pains and grief and love. Laughter, song and living - inspiration from above. So as you read each poem went into each. My prayer is that my feelings - to your heart will reach. There is a time for everything, and a po activity under the sun. A time to weep and a time to be sad, a time to laugh and a time to get mad. This book ha everything, even the bazaar, so enjoy every rhyme. like I have - so far! Kathleen J. Shields is a prolific award-w multiple genres: primarily Children's and Christian fiction. Her goal is to inspire readers through her stories (& p hopes of bringing a little extra light into the world. Poetry has always been a first-love for Kathleen. It has been since childhood. Thinking in rhyme, feeling the tune in her heart, with goals of sharing her song with others. E

Report an issue with this product or seller

Print length	Language	Publication date	Dimensions	ISBN-10
192 pages	English	October 23, 2019	5.5 x 0.48 x 8.5 inches	19413454

Read sample

The devil will take you down through pride.

As authors, we may sometimes find ourselves comparing our work to others, especially when it comes to something as visible as book reviews. It's natural to want to feel proud of our work, but when we see other books with more reviews, it can make us doubt the value or popularity of our own book.

The reality is, getting reviews can be incredibly challenging. Many authors have tons of friends who will do it for them. Other times they give away free copies of their books in exchange for reviews, but often those promises don't result in feedback. The response rate can be low, and it can feel discouraging. In an attempt to solve this problem, some authors may even consider paying for reviews, or seeking out services that offer large numbers of reviews for a price.

However, it's important to keep in mind that this practice can be risky, as reviews that aren't genuine or transparent could be flagged by Amazon, potentially leading to the removal of those reviews. While it's tempting to boost your book's visibility with positive reviews, maintaining an honest and organic approach to gaining feedback is crucial for long-term success.

The devil doesn't want to share you.

Amazon wants authors to enroll their books into KU Kindle Unlimited. This means that you must remain exclusive to Amazon's platform which might make you think twice before expanding to other platforms like Apple, Kobo, Barnes & Noble, or any other place online. But why would you do that? Why would you limit your books exposure to the world?

Free Marketing! While this may seem like a limitation, it's important to weigh the benefits of KU's marketing and exposure against the potential loss of a wider audience. Kindle Unlimited is a subscription service where readers pay $9.99 a month for access to a vast library of e-books. Authors are paid based on page reads rather than book sales, so the more a reader engages with your book, the more you earn. Additionally, every borrow counts as a sale in Amazon's algorithm, which can help improve your book's visibility.

To make the choice easier, Amazon also provides special advertising opportunities for books enrolled in Kindle Select, such as price promotions, Kindle Countdown Deals, and inclusion in Prime Reading, which can increase exposure and drive sales. These perks are free for Kindle Select authors but are only exclusive to the platform. Is it worth it? That depends on your goals as an author.

For some, the exposure and marketing tools provided by Amazon make KU an attractive option. However, I've personally found that I sell more books through Apple Books, even without heavy marketing. For authors who prioritize broad distribution, this might influence your decision to explore other platforms alongside or instead of KU.

The devil cripples you with fear.

Lately, I've seen an increasing number of authors sharing their frustrations on social media about their reviews being removed, books being taken down, or even accounts being suspended. While I can't speak to the specific reasons for these actions, I understand how deeply it can hurt after you've invested so much time and effort into publishing your book, getting the ISBN, driving traffic to your page, encouraging reviews, and even paying for advertising.

Amazon has strict policies in place to maintain the integrity of its platform, and reviews that are perceived as biased, such as paid reviews, reviews from friends and family, or those linked to fraudulent practices, are subject to removal. This is done to ensure that reviews reflect genuine customer experiences and aren't artificially inflated.

There could also be other reasons for a book or account issue. Sometimes, if the right categories or metadata weren't set up correctly when publishing, it could result in rejection. Or, if an account has been flagged for any reason related to violating Amazon's guidelines, that could lead to suspension or closure.

As an author, the best thing you can do is ensure that you're following all of Amazon's guidelines carefully and being transparent in your practices. This includes ensuring that reviews are legitimate and that your book information is accurate. And if you use AI, you acknowledge it.

Mistakes and misunderstandings can happen, but being as honest and thorough as possible can help prevent issues down the road.

The devil sidetracks you with worldly things.

Sometimes, as an author, it can feel like you're competing for attention against a whole range of other products. Amazon, after all, isn't just a bookstore—it's a massive marketplace selling everything from clothes to electronics to groceries.

So, when someone comes to look for your children's book, they're also likely to be shown ads for children's toys, clothes, and other related items. While this is part of Amazon's strategy to increase sales across various categories, it can be frustrating for authors, especially when you've worked so hard to direct potential readers to your book.

Upsells, cross-sells, and promotions are just part of Amazon's overall approach to keeping customers engaged with the site, but for an author, it can sometimes feel like a distraction that takes away from your hard-earned visibility.

The devil is the god of this world.

Amazon is without a doubt the largest force in online shopping and self-publishing today, making it nearly impossible for authors to avoid if they want to thrive in the current marketplace. With its global reach and wide range of products, Amazon has become the go-to platform for millions of consumers.

While there are other self-publishing options like Barnes & Noble Press, Draft 2 Digital, Ingram and Lulu, many of them still distribute books through Amazon. Their reach and convenience, particularly with services like free shipping for Prime members, give Amazon a significant edge that smaller platforms simply can't compete with.

As an author, you may want to print and distribute books independently, sell through your website, or partner with local stores. But here's the reality: most people you meet, when asking where they can get your book, will almost always want to know if it's available on Amazon. As long as Amazon remains as influential as it is, it's difficult to ignore the platform if you want to maximize visibility and sales.

The devil only defeats you, if you allow him to!

I know this section might have come across as dramatic, and I don't want it to discourage you. The truth is, the world of publishing—especially the part that involves giants like Amazon—can sometimes feel like navigating a minefield.

While it may seem overwhelming or even negative at times, I don't want you to walk away from your dreams. Bringing life to your story and publishing your book is still one of the most powerful and rewarding things you can do, and you absolutely deserve to have your story shared with the world.

The purpose of this section is not to scare you, but to encourage you to be aware. Don't let fear of the unknown stop you. Understand that, like any business, Amazon has its pitfalls, but it also has massive opportunities for growth.

What matters most is that you trust in your mission as an author and follow through with your calling. There is a reason why you've felt called to write and to share your story with others, and there is someone out there who needs to hear it.

Keep moving forward with courage. Be aware of the challenges, but don't let them stand in your way. Your book is important. Your voice matters. Just take care to approach this journey with wisdom.

God wants you to write! God wants your book to be put out there. And God wants your book to be read by someone specific. Make it happen.

Amazon and Other's 50+% Royalty

Amazon KDP takes as much as 50% of your book's retail price as their royalty, where Ingram requires 55% or more, leaving you with the remainder. You might be wondering: why does this matter? After all, it didn't cost you anything to publish the book. Let's break it down a bit further to see how the numbers work out.

Amazon's royalty is based on the **full retail price**, not just the profits after printing. This means they take that percentage of the total price, which includes the cost of printing. Let's look at an example to illustrate this:

Your book is priced at $10.

It costs $3 to print, leaving $7 in profit before royalties.

Let's say Amazon takes 50% of the retail price, which is $5. This leaves you with $2 in profit.

Amazon is making more money than you are, even though you're the one who created the content.

You might think, "Well, why not just raise the price of my book to make up for this?" But here's the catch: Amazon still takes their percentage off of the full retail price. So, if you raise the price by $5 to offset their cut, they would still make more than you. It's a tough reality, but it shows how much Amazon benefits from the sale compared to the author.

It's important to understand this dynamic as you plan your pricing strategy. You worked hard on your book, and it can feel frustrating to see so much of the revenue going to Amazon.

Expanded Distribution's Royalty

When you opt for **expanded distribution,** you're giving Amazon the right to distribute your book to retailers like Barnes

& Noble and others. At first glance, this may seem like a great opportunity, but the hidden costs involved can be surprising, especially when you try to do the math, it can be really hard to follow.

You might notice that your royalty from expanded distribution looks much smaller than expected, but its only 40% how does that work out?

It's important to recognize that Amazon isn't offering this service out of sheer generosity. They are still making money off your book in more ways than one.

Let's break it down with an example:

Your book retails for $10.

- Amazon takes 40% off the retail price for distribution, which is $4.

- The printing cost is $3, leaving $7 to be split.

- Amazon pays for printing ($3), and after subtracting the $4 for distribution, you're left with $1.

So, when all is said and done, Amazon receives $4 for distribution, $3 for printing, and you receive $1. But here's where it gets a little tricky—there's no clear explanation of where the rest of the money goes. Technically, Amazon takes an additional 20% of the retail price for the distribution rights, meaning they're also making an additional $2.

It may seem like Amazon is getting the bigger slice of the pie, but they are covering a lot of costs, from printing, to hosting your book on their platform. And in fairness, distribution services from other retailers or physical bookstores often take a percentage of sales as well. So while it may seem like you're earning a smaller share, remember that they are offering a comprehensive platform that handles the printing, marketing, and logistics for you.

However, here's one possible solution: If the royalty share were more balanced, with profits split after the printing cost, it would seem fairer. For example, if your book retails for $10 and printing costs $3, that leaves $7. If Amazon and the author both received 50% after printing, you'd both get $3.50. This would be a more equitable split, where both parties get compensated for their contributions without one party being overly advantaged. Unfortunately, the world doesn't work that way.

At the end of the day, Amazon benefits from the content you create. Without authors like you using their platform, they wouldn't have a product to sell. So while it's clear that Amazon profits, it's also important to remember that they're providing a platform, and distribution services that make it possible to reach readers around the world. It's a partnership—just one where the numbers may feel a little more tilted in their favor than you might expect.

Amazon Advantage Mishaps

Why use **Amazon Advantage?** Quality control for starters. There is a section detailing how POD books have massive printing issues from the ink, to the glue to the printers getting jammed and someone else's book interior getting pasted inside your book's cover.... But is this really the way to go?

I've read stories about other authors utilizing Amazon's Advantage Program, which is basically a consignment program that enables authors and publishers to sell new books, printed by any printer, through Amazon. It gives your book, printed in bulk by local or Chinese printers, an opportunity to have an Amazon product page, but with everything, there is a catch. Isn't there always?

First you pay to print your books and have them shipped to you. Yes, they are less money to produce than Print on Demand (POD) when you order 500-1000+. They are likely much better quality, in print color, paper stock and even binding. Just don't forget to include the shipping costs to that printing total.

Then you join the AA program and ship a few books (I believe it is no more than 6) to each of the Amazon warehouses (which there are 100 warehouses as of this writing) where they sit on a shelf and wait for sales. If they don't sell by a specific timeframe (at one point it was 6 weeks), they are shipped back to you at your expense, for you to then, ship back to them to start the clock again. Even with media mail costs, the price for shipping adds up substantially.

On top of that, Amazon takes 55% of the retail price. Do the math on the printing, shipping, your desired royalty and their 55% and see what your Retail price would need to be to make money. But that's not the only cost to take into account.

You must apply to join the Amazon Advantage program. Acceptance is not automatic or guaranteed and it takes one to two weeks for your application to be reviewed. If accepted, the cost is $99 per year regardless of the number of books you sell. You better hope you are selling hundreds of books in that time frame.

Additionally, it is country specific, if you are in the US you can't sell in Canada, Germany or the UK. You must have an address, bank account and the rights to sell your book in each country. Then ship books to each Amazon Warehouse in each country – trust me, this is not cost conducive in anyway – that is why POD is so popular.

On top of that, there may be issues with connecting your books to your Amazon author page making it difficult to run ads – of which I also add to that – paying Amazon for ads to promote your book that they are going to take 55% of the retail sale from, is seemingly not cost effective.

There ARE a few benefits to this, like, if you package your book with other things like bookmarks or toys, you can sell them together, but remember this if you are paying for shipping back and forth. Media mail rate is only good for the book, not the additional products.

You CAN list your book for preorder, something KDP can't do for print books yet, which is beyond my understanding. And your book product page looks exactly like a book distributed by a major publisher. It shows "sold and shipped by Amazon" members get Prime free shipping and you can still use the A+ content feature to jazz up your product page.

But I am fairly certain if you put together a pro-con list, you will hesitate going this route…. Unless your kickstarter campaign banked you thousands!

The 5 biggest complaints about Amazon Advantage

1. **Multiple ship-to locations.** Amazon has more than 100 fulfillment centers in the United States alone. This can make it challenging for a self-publisher with one or just a few books to manage. One day you might get an order to send three books to location X, and two days later to send one book to location Y. You need to ship those ASAP because Amazon gives you a window during which they expect the books. Your performance in this regard is measured and scored and your account may be penalized, or worse.

2. **Damaged books.** You must make sure the books are packaged such that they arrive undamaged and in pristine condition. Any damaged books—even a bent corner on the cover—may result in the book being returned, and at your expense.

3. **Returns.** Let's say your book has a lot of pre-orders, or there is a sudden surge of orders. Amazon's inventory algorithm will ask you to ship them books based on their forecast of customer demand. If demand falls off and they decide they have too much inventory, they start returning books. Again, this is at your expense, and worse: returns can dribble in over the course of time rather than all at once.

4. **Storing inventory.** You most likely printed an inventory of books so now you need a place to store them while waiting for orders.

5. **Shipping costs.** Most self-publishers don't have the shipping volumes to qualify for shipping discounts. USPS Media Mail rates are usually the only way to preserve a profit margin. But delivery dates are hard to predict, and vary, so this method of shipping may not get the books there in time (see #1). Shipping costs can quickly erode anticipated profits.

Amazon Seller Central as an alternative to Amazon Advantage?

The primary alternative to Amazon Advantage is Amazon Seller Central, sometimes known as Marketplace. You act as the retailer, essentially advertising your book on Amazon. When a customer buys your book, Amazon holds the payment while you ship the order to the customer.

Seller Central can be used to sell new or used books. But you are competing with anyone else selling your book. You may decide your book's price, but not the information on the product detail page as you do with Amazon Advantage. You are competing with anyone that has a copy of your book. When you see a product and there are alternative prices and it says "from other sellers" that's this.

The Cost of Seller Central/Marketplace

Amazon Seller Central has two programs: Individual and Professional.

- The individual plan charges $0.99 per item, plus 15% of the item's price (referral fee), plus a closing fee of $1.80 per book. Importantly, Amazon provides a reimbursement of shipping fees according to a schedule.

- The professional plan has several marketing and selling features designed for those selling 40 or more books per month. The monthly charge is $39.99. The referral fee of 15% and closing fee of $1.80 apply here as well, as does the reimbursement of shipping fees.

Marketing with Seller Central

While using Seller Central, your book is shown to shoppers when they search for it. However, even though you are the publisher, your book will be displayed as available from a third-party seller, which might not be as appealing to some customers. On the bright side, with Seller Central, you retain control over your book's pricing, which can be critical if you wish to maintain consistent pricing for your distributors.

What is Fulfillment By Amazon (FBA)?

An alternative to you doing the shipping is using Amazon's Fulfillment by Amazon, FBA. With FBA, you ship books to an Amazon warehouse and Amazon fulfills customer orders, thus making your book available for Prime shipping.

Fulfillment by Amazon (FBA) is a program that lets you outsource order fulfillment to Amazon and offer customers free, two-day shipping through Prime. By enrolling in FBA, you can send your products into Amazon's global network of fulfillment centers, and we'll pick, pack, and ship orders, as well as handle customer service and returns. FBA is part of a fully automated set of services called Supply Chain by Amazon.

Costs for FBA depend on the products you sell and the exact services you use. Inventory storage costs are charged monthly based on the daily average volume (measured in cubic feet) for the space your inventory occupies in Amazon fulfillment centers. However, you are also charged monthly for all items stored in a fulfillment center for more than 181 days.

While this option mainly applies to those who are selling products other than books, it is an option. And if all of this isn't enough to confuse you as to which route to go, you will want to research and compare everything as details and programs change constantly.

Plus, programs get renamed, and new programs can be created.

--------------------〜〜◯----------------------

My take away: if you are just starting out in the self-publishing world, still hold a day job, don't have a huge savings account to live off and don't want to make this into a full-time business, go the print-on-demand route and just master marketing and work on writing your next book.

Algorithms & Associations

What is an algorithm? An algorithm is a set of rules or a process followed to solve problems or perform calculations, typically by a computer. Search engines like Google use algorithms to determine which websites appear on the first page of results. Social media platforms like Facebook have algorithms that filter what posts you see based on your interactions. Similarly, Amazon has algorithms that determine which products are most popular and are shown to customers.

Unfortunately, these algorithms are often designed to benefit the companies that create them. For example, Google's algorithm is designed to make it harder for your website to be found, even if you're using the right keywords. You might not show up in search results unless you explicitly search for the website by name. The same happens on Amazon. You can search for the exact title of your book, and sometimes, it won't show up unless you also include your author name.

Why does this happen? Because the algorithm is designed this way. Amazon, like Google and Facebook, wants you to pay for ads to get your product in front of customers. Without ads, you're left to figure out how to gain visibility in a system that prioritizes the most popular products. These products sit at the top of the search results, just beneath the sponsored listings. Once they make it to the top, they tend to stay there because that's what customers see first.

So, how do you beat the algorithm, especially when it changes every few months? Unfortunately, there's no easy answer. Suggesting that paying for advertisements is the solution just leads to another issue: paying distribution fees, covering printing costs, and receiving small royalties. This is tough for authors who don't have deep pockets.

In a system like this, the odds are stacked against you. Your chances of success are lower, especially when you're working with limited funds. But that doesn't mean you can't win some battles. Your relationships and associations can influence your chances.

What do I mean by associations? I'm referring to any entity besides yourself that's involved in the creation, distribution, or presentation of your book. One of the most important of these is the printer. Whether you use KDP, Ingram, or Draft2Digital, printing errors do happen. Paper jams, low ink, manufacturing delays, and shipping issues are all common. Mistakes happen, but fortunately, the associated companies typically make it right.

However, don't expect priority service. If a mistake is made, and you go through the process to prove it, they may reprint your order and send it to you. But even then, you still won't get priority. It could take another

10 business days or more to get your books printed and delivered. And that's just for your own inventory.

What about when people order books online and receive a misprint? They don't think to themselves oh KDP or Ingram didn't print it properly and messed up. No, they think something's wrong with the author. They leave reviews that are not five-star. Even though Amazon is trying to cut down on people leaving reviews for shipping issues, it still happens.

Just yesterday I read a one-star review for a product and the review was that they delivered the wrong product. It had nothing to do with the product at all! It had everything to do with the delivery mistake, but that one star review is still there, and is affecting the person's five-star rating. There is not much you can do about that but keep track of daily reviews and bring it to their attention. I mean what else do you have to do with your time?

- I've received books where the cover was mine, but the interior was somebody else's book.

- I've received books where the cover was mine, the interior was mine, but the cover was put on upside down.

- I've received books that were thicker than they should have been because a second book was bound inside.

- I've received books where the first book had beautiful color, and the last book was all faded or you could tell that the printer ran out of yellow, or magenta.

- I've received books where there must have been a jam in the printer, and half the pages are sideways or at a diagonal, or cut off.

- I've received books that were not cut properly, and the pages were stuck together.

- I've also received books where they used too much glue on the binding and so the pages were stuck together.

- I've received inventory where the box was drenched.

- I've received a box of inventory that didn't have enough packaging inside and the books shifted during shipment, and the pages and covers were crumpled.

Those are just some of the issues I've had with the inventory that I've received. Now imagine what your readers are going to get when they order something online. Do you think every book that goes out the door is perfect?

All of that affects your customer's outlook on your book, and absolutely none of it has anything to do with you or your story. This is why so many people try to avoid working with distributors, ordering large quantities of books from China and doing the distribution themselves, but do you know what? There are still shipping issues on both ends so not all of these mistakes can be avoided. They happen, at no fault of your own.

I read a story about an author who was using a printer that did a poor job in packaging and was clearly at fault when the entire order was ruined during transit. The printing company adamantly refused to acknowledge any responsibility, rudely blaming the shipping company, and refused to reprint the order.

With no other recourse, the author took to social media to educate others about this company's unscrupulous behavior and that's when the story got worse!

A few days later, after hundreds had seen and responded to her post, she removed her post and replaced it with a canned response that; *they were going to fix the issue.*

With an inquiry direct to the author it was evident that "The only way they would agree to replace the damaged books was if she took down the post and update that they replaced the inventory." Her words.

If you think that seems fair, think again – that iss **Blackmail!**

My latest order took 22 days to print. Should have been 10, and I got every excuse under the moon, and it was not even holiday time (meaning there are extreme delays due to excessive orders). I was one day away from not having inventory for a trade show when I ordered them a month in advance. These things happen and there is nothing you can do about it.

Since COVID, 2020, my printer and distributor removed their phone number, and their chat option from their website. They just recently added their email addresses back in a place that you could easily find them. Can you imagine, not being able to call and talk to a human being when you want a quick answer?

Nope, you wait for an email response. And I've waited over a week before receiving a reply.

And here's the kicker, these algorithms, these associations, these errors and issues and delays and non-communication, are not only something you have to just put up with, you can't even threaten to go somewhere else. The idea of taking that business away from them and going somewhere that might appreciate you more, might sound satisfying but it is not realistic in the slightest!

First, there are not very many options out there. Not for self-publishers. Oh sure, you could bulk print and distribute yourself, do you really want to do that?

You've already paid for the interior and cover file uploads and the annual distribution fees through Ingram, so that money would be down the drain. You would have to walk away from all of those setup fees for every book you have up there.

You would also have to purchase and use all new ISBNs because the other places are going to see that the previous number is being or has already been used.

Same book, same cover, same everything, but they are too cookie-cutter to accept the same ISBN. You will lose your sales rankings. You will lose your product page and reviews. And you will lose all that money.

Not including the time and effort of unpublishing and republishing, redesigning covers for new printers, etc.

So, you are stuck there. No matter how angry you get. No matter how much you want to take your business elsewhere. You can threaten, but they know they've got you by the short hairs and they like it!

And with that little bit of knowledge right there, that is enough to lead you to the next section.

Book Marketing, a Full-Time Job

One of the most challenging aspects of publishing that many authors overlook is the sheer amount of work involved in marketing your book. You might think that writing the book or even getting it published is the hardest part, but the truth is, marketing your book is the real challenge.

You need to start marketing long before your book is released. Building a fan base, generating buzz, and getting people excited for your book's future release is key to its success. And even once it's published, the marketing doesn't stop there. It's a continuous effort to keep your book in the public's eye, pushing for attention and sales at every turn.

Before the book's release, your marketing efforts are all about exposure. You'll need to secure editorial reviews, plan social media campaigns, and create anticipation. Then, when the big release day arrives, you might think, *"That's it. Now my book will sell itself."* But that's rarely the case. After the launch, more marketing is required: additional social media pushes, more reviews, advertisements, and publicity. You'll likely be booking yourself into book events, festivals, and shows.

You'll spend your time crafting press releases, reaching out to promotional groups, and contacting schools, libraries, and bookstores. But here's the catch: it's all done one bookstore, one library, one school, and one event at a time. This can be incredibly time-consuming. Between these marketing tasks, you'll find it nearly impossible to carve out time for writing the next book, or even maintaining your day job and personal life.

Book marketing truly is a full-time job.

If you want to be an "authorpreneur"—an author plus entrepreneur—you need to dedicate time each day, week, or month to promoting your book. Without consistent self-promotion, your book can quickly become stagnant. It can sit on the virtual shelf with little-to-no sales, eventually being forgotten.

A self-published book, however, can continue to build momentum over time, *if* you consistently promote it. But be warned: many readers and industry professionals look at how long a book has been out and may question its success if it hasn't sold well in its first few years.

Remember, legitimate book contests typically only accept books published within the past year. You can't submit a book that's been out for multiple years and expect to be considered. To succeed, you need to be prepared to invest the time, effort, and budget to market your book effectively during its first year.

Just because your book didn't fly off the shelves in its first year doesn't mean it isn't a great book or that you aren't successful. It just means that your marketing didn't reach as many people as you had hoped.

With book number two, you'll need to double down on your efforts—everything you did for the first book, plus more.

And if you think that sounds exhausting,
try doing it for 40+ books
and keeping it going for 25 years...

While writing more books and working 2 jobs.

Promotion & Marketing Websites

This could almost be put in the scammers section though I felt it needed its own section as there are so many. Free ones that focus on authors only and have no real readers. Paid ones that take a small amount but still don't really get you exposure and expensive ones that may or may not help at all because, let's face it, they are trying to gain authors who will pay for their books to be promoted but do very little marketing to readers. Of course, some would say, authors ARE readers, but really, when you, as an author, check out these websites, why are you there? To buy books or to promote your own?

Additionally, you may think, so what, I'll add my book to the free ones. Sure, you can, and I have to quite a few over the years, thinking that it will help your book by showing more websites that have it. Yes and no. At the time a decade ago, Google's algorithms helped your exposure. But they've changed their algorithms and websites without traffic and pages without interest simply don't get shown.

That's when they tell you for only $5 you can be prominently displayed on the home page. That's cheap right? Why not, right? Of course, that is what every author thinks. 20 authors later, your front-page listing is now on page 2 again. Pay another $5 – it's cheap! How many times will you fall for that? Again, remembering that only authors are visiting that site.

Press Release

Only if its news worthy!** Seriously think about this. You are watching the evening news, or the morning news shows. When they DO discuss books and talk with authors, who are they talking to? Celebrities? New York Times Best Sellers?

The dream is to have an interview on a national morning show, or a daytime talk show. Thousands of people hear about your book all at once. The reality is getting an interview on your local morning news broadcast. But how do you do that? You write something that is newsworthy. Not just the book, but the press release as well.

I've said it before and I'll say it again, the "I wrote a children's book" title and article is not going to get that press release any traction. I wrote a book to address the problem of bullying – that gains attention.

So if you want to do a press release, write one that is truly news-worthy, then promote it on those PR websites and see how it goes.

Movie Producers & Screen Writers

The next big dream is to have your book made into a movie. Of course, not the movie that everyone walks away from saying "the book was better" but even at that, the fact that your book was made into a movie is still a dream worth aspiring to – realistically.

First, is that book, movie-worthy? Would it do well as a movie, tv series or show? Answer that honestly. Just because you love it, and your family says they love it, will the rest of the world love it?

How is it doing in sales? If it is sitting stagnant and hasn't seen any sales in a while and someone emails you saying they want to make the book into a movie – no matter how thrilling the idea may be ask yourself, WHY? Why would they want to spend years writing a screenplay, promoting it to their investors and developing the movie if no one is willing to buy the book? I know that sounds harsh, but the harsh reality is, they are likely planning on scamming you out of your money – likely to pay for them to write the screenplay that will attract the producers. And then, just a little more to get their agents to knock on those movie producers doors – erh emails.

That being said, I signed a contract with an agent of the movie rights for one of my children's books. I don't know if it will ever come to fruition, but they have 3 years to see if they can do something with it. And it didn't cost me a thing. That's how it's done.

PS – it still takes years after that. The writing. The investors. The promise to film And then the actual filming. Editing. And big release. If anyone tells you it could happen quick, they are lying.

Returns and Refunds

V**iral Tik-Tok Challenges** that do more harm than good... One of the latest scams includes purchasing e-books, reading them, and then returning them care of Amazon's 14-day return policy. It was a new book tok trend that was making waves in the bookish community for all the wrong reasons. The current trend and the major discussion moving forward on all social media platforms was how to save money and continue to read for free.

There are hopes that Amazon is going to rework their rules in regards to returns, especially for eBooks that have been read all the way to the end, but as of yet, it is not happened.

Amazon's policy states that readers can get a full refund for a book if it's returned within the time frame specified even if they have read the book completely.

This feature is only to be used for accidental purchases or have if you have genuine complaints regarding the book; like formatting errors or book being unreadable, however with the surge in returns of books Amazon needs to put in place a system to weed out false returns or scammers because that's what people are doing.

If you buy an eBook read it and enjoy it, then you should not be able to return it because it is unethical. It's also incredibly harmful to authors! But people don't think that way. They think it is an e-book. It doesn't cost the author anything. It only cost you how many years of your life and how much money to develop and edit... And of course you are banking on the money made from sales to, oh I don't know, pay your bills, pay for marketing, maybe quit your day job.

This abuse of the refund policy also takes away the author's royalties. Say you buy a book, the author receives a royalty payment for the sale. You return the book, the authors royalties are deducted.

But then there's something else that nobody is taking into consideration. The delivery fee of that eBook. Amazon is not going to absorb that cost, no matter how big they are. They also deduct that from the author's royalties. Well, it is not much per eBook, but it adds up. Eventually the authors royalties go into the negative and they end up paying Amazon instead of the other way around. Please don't do that. We've already spent our life savings cultivating these books and marketing them. Our royalties are literally pennies on the dollar and we've already been conned by decades worth of movies that show successful authors being rich beyond their wildest dreams and dodging adoring fans at every street corner.

This problem is not exclusive to just Amazon eBooks, it's also on Audible, and their policy is even worse. They offer you returns up to a year of your purchase even after fully listening to the audiobook.

I mean seriously, if somebody wants to read a book for free or hear an audiobook for free, they need to check out the library services that also offer eBooks and audio books. And the good thing about the library services, is when they purchase an eBook or an audiobook they purchase a certain number of loan rights. And if the book ends up being popular, they have to buy more rights to it. It's not just a buy it once and give it away for free indefinitely.

Even with library eBooks you still have an opportunity to make money. But when big retailers like Amazon and Audible offer free returns, and people are taking advantage of it, this is about as close as you can get to pirating a book, because the only one making money is the company offering your hard work for free.

---

*As of this printing, I have heard that there are efforts being made to track eBook reads and if the book has been read more than 10% Amazon may decline the return. But if someone wants to deceive the system, they can likely figure out a way, eventually.

Scammers!

S cammers come in all forms and faces. From phishing calls to fake emails to terrifying pop-ups on websites and letters that look like bills in the mail. Once you copyright your work or mention your upcoming book on social media, the scammers will literally crawl out of the woodwork ready to chomp into their next meal.

Unethical business practices, most focused on extracting money from authors are prolific. They will offer to sell you services, marketing, reviews, websites, publishing deals, movie opportunities and so much more. Here's a little of what to look out for.

Fake Copyrights

This category is just disgusting. Companies that charge excessive fees to copyright your work. They play on your vulnerabilities, scare you with plagiarism and legalities and then offer you solutions that are quick and easy and all it costs you is a ton of money.

$500 Annual copyright renewal – yes, I know an author who was scammed with this one. They didn't think anything of the $500 price tag but when the bill came in to pay again the following year, his red flags went up. By then we didn't even know if it was legitimately copyrighted so we had to research and duplicate his efforts.

$1800 Legal fees for copyright - That's right, they try to sell people on the legalities of copyrighting.

"When publishing on major platforms, having Copyright Legalities is essential for several reasons:

Legal Ownership: Copyright legalities establish you as the legal owner of your work, preventing others from using, selling, or distributing it without permission.

Revenue Protection: Copyright ensures that only you can profit from your book, preventing others from illegally earning off your work.

Content Security on Platforms: Copyright legalities protection ensures that platforms recognize you as the original creator, discouraging unauthorized distribution or duplication by others.

Without proper protection, your book may face the following threats:

Unauthorized Reproduction: Others may copy or distribute your work without consent, impacting your earnings.

Plagiarism: Unprotected content can be claimed or repurposed by others as their own.

Piracy: Digital versions of your book may be illegally distributed online.

Loss of Credibility: Lack of ownership proof can challenge your legitimacy as the original creator.

Filing of Lawsuit: You can only file a lawsuit in case of infringement if you have complete documentation on your end.

This process includes a fixed cost of $1800, which will be paid to the Attorney General to secure the copyright registration."

But if you just read that and thought that seemed justifiable – I have a bridge in Arizona to sell you.

The likelihood that your content will be pirated is slim, unless it does very well. If it does get pirated, it will be overseas in a country that does not have copyright relations and treaties.

"There is no such thing as an "international copyright" that will automatically protect an author's writings throughout the world. Protection against unauthorized use in a particular country depends on the national laws of that country."

Hiring a lawyer and filing a lawsuit is going to cost you tens of thousands of dollars at a minimum of $350 per billable hour for an attorney. That is, IF you can find an attorney willing to go after the unknown entities that pirated or plagiarized your work. And the likelihood you will make it to court, and win, and see a payment from them is about as likely as catching the moon with a stick.

Just go to copyright.gov and figure out their convoluted system. It costs $55 (was $35) and lasts your entire life plus 70 years. If you can't figure it out, maybe you can hire someone to do it for you, but will they do it right? Will you get the certificate? Who gets notified of issues and changes? Seriously, you are a writer. You research how to dispose of bodies in murder mysteries, look into the amount of sulfites in wine for your vineyard romance and read up on what it was like in the old west for your historical fiction – so read the instructions and make sure you do it.

Copyright Crawlers

Like cockroaches in the kitchen... Did you know that after you have paid your money to copyright.gov to officially copyright your hard work and protect it from plagiarists and thieves, they put your information on a list of newly copyrighted books and allow anyone to purchase that mailing list? Nice right? All of a sudden you begin getting emails and phone calls from 'publishers and agents' who have 'heard great things' about your work, and want to 'offer you a publishing deal' and it'll only cost...

When vanity publishers start contacting you regarding your book (that they don't reference a title to) and offering you the moon, that is your first clue. Real publishers are inundated with submissions via agents or via unsolicited manuscripts. They have zero time to ambulance chance a new wanna-be author.

But it doesn't stop there. They also check the lists of older copyrights. Those that are over 5 or even 10 years old. They contact those authors as well. Why, you ask? Because you've likely given up. You feel like a failure, and you are easy pickin's for the vultures. They will swoop in, and offer a deal to make it even better, give it new life, and if you are willing to make a deal with the devil (or an alchemist) you will spend more than you initially did to kick a dead horse.

Wicked Websites

From website clones, to those designed to record your keystrokes, get you to login to other accounts or buy something they don't actually sell, the types of wicked websites out there is plentiful. When I was first teaching myself how to create websites, I used Microsoft FrontPage with Internet Explorer and found that I could open any webpage on IE into Frontpage and see the HTML code that was used to write the design. I could save as the page, modify the text and images and have a fully designed page ready to launch on my own server.

I read the code and learned how to make my own websites this way. Of course, so did the hackers which is why HTML5, CSS, JavaScript, jQuery, CSS, ASP and PHP all eventually replaced it. Each form of code was a new attempt at keeping hackers out of websites, of creating more secure sites. While I couldn't keep up with the new codes, the same theory applies.

Why do I mention this? I've entered websites that were low-resolution screenshots of legitimate websites with very few pages but plenty of ways to buy a cheap item and enter your credit card details. They do this with defunct or bankrupt and out-of-business book publishers and literary agents too.

I have been on the receiving end of really well-written emails from 'legitimate agents or publishers, with names I have heard of in the industry, only to discover that the domain name expired and was repurchased and launched a month or two ago. They went to those cached websites, copied what the old site looked like and the text that was on it, and modified it to send out to unsuspecting targets.

How do you find out if it's a new fake site? You can type any domain name into a who.is search and it will tell you how long it has been active, when it expired and when it was renewed. I think my favorite thing to note is when a company says it has been in the industry for a decade but the domain name is three months old. Really? That brings me to faux's and phishers.

Faux's and Phishers

Temptation is what they do, preying on the **eager is how they win.** It is easy to be tempted by solicitations for quick and easy publishing or agents. Tread carefully when it comes to unsolicited invitations to submit. With a little investigation, though, you can avoid such publishing scams. All you need to do is type the name of the company into a search with the word scam or review. If they've burned people, there will be information about it.

There was one I received from a literary management company's top exec seeking information under the guise of a representation offer. It was well written; said everything it was supposed to and even used a deceptively similar mailing address.

They want you to submit your outline, query letter, manuscript or business plan... to what end? Who knows? To steal your hard work? To submit it on your behalf and get a deal instead of you? Who knows. I cannot think like them and I wouldn't want to.

———————————————◁≫◁○————————————————

Film Studio Frauds

A studio wants to make my book into a movie! I've seen emails come in from Sony Pictures, TriStar Pictures, Lionsgate and CBS Studios offering film adaptations. Key indicators of the scam include a Gmail email address like the following: (acquisition.tristarpictures@gmail.com), rather than an official TriStar or Sony domain email address like *aquisitions@sony.com*

The FBI's Los Angeles Field Office has issued a report on financial fraud schemes targeting authors by impersonating film production studios. The report warns production studios and publishers that scammers are emailing authors impersonating real or fake executives at their companies.

The report included scam indicators to watch out for, such as:

- Names that don't correspond to actual employees.
- Email domains that don't correspond to a company's legitimate domain name.

- Phone numbers or email addresses that don't match a legitimate employee's published contact information.
- Requests for funds.

Amazon Copycats

Amazon **KDP has had to file lawsuits** against companies falsely claiming to be affiliated with Amazon. Victims believe they are working with Amazon, paying "substantial sums of money, often thousands of dollars, for grossly inadequate or non-existent services.

There are book festival scams, offering the biggest book festival in (insert big name city here). *"For $XXX.00 we can add your book to a bookshelf."* Your book will be lost among thousands of others. Plus, there is always the chance that the company may not even bother to display it. If you are not there to check, how will you know?

Or, you can pay to be at this festival, send your check to this private mailbox in Los Angeles and fly out in six months to discover that your name is not on the list. I remember typing the mailing address into a Google search, doing street view and seeing a run-down shopping center in a rough part of town. Yeah, that looks legitimate to me.

Unsolicited Callers

Do not trust any business proposition that comes from an unsolicited phone call. They are not trying to help you by selling you an extended warranty. Your bill cannot be paid with a Walmart gift card. And the IRS will never call and ask you to verify your social security number.

If anyone claiming they are in the book industry calls you out of the blue offering you the sky – and your book is not already selling thousands per month – they are scamming you.

- Do they even know the title of your book?
- Do they even know what it is about?

They are almost always offering to republish it under their umbrella. Why? It's already available. Or they are going to offer you expensive marketing services that will cost you every step of the way. Pay me for the idea, then pay me to create the marketing item, then pay me to keep track of the sales for you.

You already have access to a plethora of marketing ideas on the internet, you don't need them to tell you that you need a book trailer video, you now know. You don't need them to write the script for the video because you know your book better than them and you know what you want the people to see in that video. You may need help creating that video if you don't have the skills, but you can supply exactly what you want including the text, images and videos so any videographer can create it quickly and cheaply.

I took a call from one of these scammers and they offered me marketing services for my book. I, as many of you are wondering, what can we do to better to market our books, kept the conversation going. I was truly curious as to what they claimed to be offering authors that maybe I hadn't thought about yet.

Here's the conversation in a nutshell:

"Do you have a book trailer video?"

"I do," I responded.

"Do you have an ecommerce website to sell books on?"

"That's my day job," I acknowledged.

"Do you have a social media presence?"

"Yuppers," I confirmed.

"Have you created flyers and done mailings?"

"I am a graphic designer, so yes."

"Have you entered book contests?"

"Definitely," I declared. "And won many!"

"Have you written a press release?"

"Absolutely," I boasted. "Many distributed by contests after I won their awards."

"Have you done news interviews?"

"I have, when I won those awards." I gushed.

"Have you done Facebook ad campaigns, Google advertisements and/or Amazon marketing?"

"Unfortunately…" I admitted.

He put me on hold. He went to his boss to ask what else he could offer. After a couple of minutes, he came back and said there was nothing they could do to help me. Haha. Apparently, I had done everything they know how to charge you for, and I am still where I am in my marketing efforts.

*Note I didn't say the word "Yes." While I have heard that they can use a recording of you saying the word Yes to agree to sign up for things you didn't agree to, I don't know how valid that story is. Just be careful and cautious.

It's not you. It's not your book. It's not the lack of marketing funds. It's the fact that the book world is overly saturated with new books. The average person doesn't read, or if they do, they truly can't read millions of books in a year. It's the fact that most people have budgets and can't afford to buy as many books as they want. And if that wasn't enough, add in the algorithms that keep your content from being discoverable without paying for expensive ads. It's truly a dark world you are trying to rise up in.

You know, God never intended for us to become superstars. He never expected us to reach every person spanning across the globe. We were only designed to share our talents and stories with those around us, our community, our village, our town.

There is a verse in the bible: **1 Peter 4:10** (NIV), which encourages us to use our gifts to serve others:

> *"Each of you should use whatever gift you have received to serve others, as faithful stewards of God's grace in its various forms."*

This emphasizes that our gifts are meant to be used in service to others, not necessarily for fame or recognition, but to build up and help those around us.

It is the devil who has warped our thinking of this world to feel like we are failures if we are not household names and millionaires. Don't base your success on your piggy bank or sales ranking.

Instead, base your success on a smile on a readers face, a sale that requests an autograph, a sale of your second book that you didn't see coming, a five-star review that comes out of nowhere, a returning customer, a signup on your blog or website, a child who remembers your school visit from years ago, a parent who refers you to their child's school, a bookstore that asks you for a signing, an award won over hundreds of other submissions, an article written or an interview shared, a referral from a friend or anything else that helps you see the positivity of what you have accomplished.

Your God-given talent was given to you to share. And when God wants that story read by specific people, He will make sure they find it. You just have to do the work to make sure it is findable when the time comes.

Social Media Attention

Posts **on social media attract attention.** That could be good. That could be bad. If they say congratulations; smile and be appreciative. If they offer to be your friend, ask for a DM or gush about your book and then ask what genre you write, be cautious, as they are likely spammers.

Check their profile. Is it new? Is it active? Does it state they are marketers? If they offer to DM you, they are likely going to try to sell you something. If they ask you to send them a friend request, ask why? Why can't they send their own request?

When you see posts that state: "Authors post your book cover or book link here." Ask yourself, why?

Sure, you can do it, but who's looking at that feed? Authors. They are posting their link. Do they even care about your link? Probably not. Are they your ideal readers? Probably not.

- What are they going to do with that link?
- How does it benefit their social media statistics?

They are gaining monetary credits on active and viral posts with a ton of comments. Think about it.

Plagiarism & Copyright Infringement

Fear of your work being plagiarized is real. If you copyright your work, you don't have to worry as much. If you send out PDF's of your ARC, put a watermark across the pages. If you spot your book or a similar-looking book on Amazon, you can report it. If you find it overseas, there are steps you can take to rectify it. The importance is in knowing the difference between plagiarism and copyright infringement and simple distribution.

Plagiarism and copyright infringement are different but related forms of intellectual property misuse. Plagiarism is **presenting someone else's work as your own, without giving proper credit.** It is an ethical violation that often occurs in academic settings. Copyright infringement is **using a copyrighted work**, like a book, **without the author's permission or the law's exception**. It is a legal violation that can result in penalties.

In the world of self-publishing, many writers are seeing their work being appropriated without their permission. Some books are copied word-for-word while others are tinkered with just enough to make it tough for an automated plagiarism checker to flag them. The offending books often stay up for weeks or even months at a time before they're detected, usually by an astute reader.

For the author, this intrusion goes beyond threatening their livelihood. Writing a novel is a form of creative expression, and having it stolen by someone else, many say, can feel like a personal violation.

Speaking of personal violations – here's a screen capture of an email I received shortly after releasing my How To book – this was a nice, peaceful way to start my morning...

> WRITE, MARKET AND SELL
> CHILDREN'S BOOKS WILL BE ON
> PIRATEBAY AND PLAGIARISED
> WITH AI SOON!
>
> **ANONYMOUS** 8h
> Bcc: You
> More Details
>
> PLUS YOUR PERSONAL INFO GIVEN TO
> LOCAL THUGS IN YOUR AREA! YES WE
> KNOW WHO YOU ARE AND WHERE YOU
> LIVE. STOP YOUR GOODREADS AND SOCIAL
> MEDIA PROMOTIONS IF YOU DON'T WANT IT
> TO HAPPEN! WE DON'T LIVE IN YOUR
> COUNTRY AND YOUR LAWS CAN DO
> NOTHING TO US!

Yes, I reported it to the FBI but you know nothing happened to them. Just like credit card fraud, stolen identity and now mortgage scams that you are responsible for even though you did nothing wrong.

My book is for sale on other websites.

This is not the same as plagiarism and copyright infringement. "I saw my book for sale on Walmart or eBay and I didn't put it there." Distribution offers that book to anyone willing to put it on their platform. They get the sale, they make their fee for putting it on the web and you get the sale, funneled to your book distributor/printer as royalties paid monthly. An online bookstore is selling my book but the retail price is more than I set, why? Because they can. Will they get the sale? Who knows. Will you get the royalties? Yes.

Amazon marked my book down to pennies over my print cost (or less). What do I do? Embrace it. This means they have physical copies on their warehouse shelves taking up space and they are trying to get rid of them quickly. That means they purchased them a couple of months ago and you received the royalties for them already. They just want to make their out-of-pocket money back and save themselves the shipping cost to send them back to the distributor.

Offer them to your fans as a special short-term deal. "Super special deal while inventory lasts!" It will help with your sales rank and possibly get you a verified review. Either that, or buy them yourself as inventory, which helps with your sales rank. I've bought many books at print cost or less and got them faster than ordering author copies. Or, if you don't do either, get ready to receive them back as returns. If you didn't agree to pay for returns, the royalties from those sales will be deducted from future royalties.

Now, there are times you will find your autographed book for sale on eBay or on the shelves of Half Price Books or Thrift Books. No, you do not get royalties paid for those sales and it sucks. But it is the same idea as buying designer clothes at a thrift shop. You only get the sale once.

Meta used my book to train its AI program

That's not fair! I didn't get paid.... The Atlantic did an article detailing how Meta (Facebook) used our books to teach its AI – you can search for your name and find out if one of your books was used without your permission. I know authors who found ALL of their books listed. I only had one book used. The Creation of Kaitlyn Jones, the first book of my young adult trilogy.

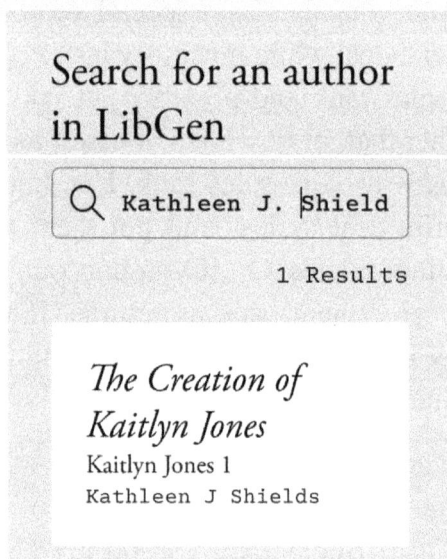

⌂   🔒 theatlantic.com   ☰   ② ⋮

Search for an author in LibGen

🔍 Kathleen J. Shield

1 Results

The Creation of Kaitlyn Jones
Kaitlyn Jones 1
Kathleen J Shields

I have a feeling that some time down the road there may be a lawsuit and there may be a settlement, but as of right now, you just get to know that your hard work was used to train a computer to write which could eventually take away your job, your talent, your dreams – and in which other unscrupulous author-wannabes who don't have talent can now have AI write a book for them to sell without having an inkling of a unique idea anywhere in their heads.

How does that make you feel?

Image Copyright Scams

Another big scam is receiving a letter from a law firm claiming the image on your website, blog, or worse, your book cover, is being used without the photographer's permission. If you have used copyrighted images without permission, either get permission or replace them with images that do not require attribution or permission.

Simply removing the offending content should be enough to satisfy the real copyright holder. Don't ever respond to the letter or email. If it is a phishing scam, it will do you no good.

Now, if the image is on your book cover... verify that this is not a scam. Locate the image in a reverse photo lookup. Find the original photographer. Determine if the email is from them or a lawyer they retained or if it is representing someone else.

Copyright trolls are a real thing. They hunt down unlicensed content and threaten legal action against copyright infringers. They often send settlement letters demanding payment to avoid going to court. These are usually hollow threats, but not always. If you don't have any copyrighted images or other content on your site that you're using without permission, then you have nothing to worry about and can safely ignore the threat. If you don't know, change it out.

Additionally, if they do not reference the details of which image is being used illegally, they are likely phishing. By not providing you the image they are hoping you will contact them to ask and they have you.

A real lawyer does not want to waste their time answering questions that could have been answered in his/her initial correspondence.

There are many helpful websites that will keep these lists updated with the latest scams they discover. Authors Guild, Predators and Editors, Poets and Writers, heck, even Reedsy provides lists of things to look out for. Just search and find out what is out there.

As scammers realize the old scams no longer work, they will invent new ways to deceive you. Just like authors invent new worlds and villains. As long as there is a will, there will be a way.

Finally, if you thought the scammers were problematic, just wait until you get into the discrimination practices, all-around rejections, computer algorithms and everything else stacked against you that will cause depression and imposter syndrome amongst other emotional dilemmas.

Goodreads Print Book Giveaways

Those **hese were once a good way to get reviews,** but way too many book re-sellers are gaming Goodreads giveaways to get free inventory. After paying the Goodreads fee, plus postage, authors not only don't get reviews, but they see their signed books for sale online later.

Of course, there are still good, honest people who ask for Goodreads giveaway books and write lovely, thoughtful reviews. But they are becoming more and more scarce. If you are going to do a giveaway, consider an eBook, it won't cost you anything. Or give a print book to a single winner.

To give out review copies, try Booksprout, Hidden Gems, NetGalley or BookFunnel. Goodreads doesn't have enough moderation, and it has devolved into a site that's toxic for authors and reviewers alike.

And remember that any unknown person who piles on generic praise for "your book" (especially when you've published many, like me) is very likely a scammer. Especially if they say they "stumbled upon" your book.

Always ask where they got their copy. If they 'hem and haw' with their answer, they're waving a big red flag. If they respond with Amazon, that's a given, 90+% come from Amazon, what drew their attention to it? A review? A referral? Or an old mailing list?

AI is Coming for You

I hesitate to put a section in the dark side of publishing regarding AI as it is likely here to stay. I have unfortunately, read numerous magazine articles and newsletters in the past year talking about all the ways that you, as an author, can use AI to benefit yourself and your work.

People are using AI to come up with story ideas. Plots. They are using AI to help them come up with book titles, fantasy world names and world descriptions. They're using AI to create their illustrations for free. It's being used to edit, check grammar, rewrite sections and translate. They are using AI to figure out their keyword phrases, social media campaigns and to write copy for their websites.

While I don't like the use of AI as I feel like it is taking away the little bits of humanity we still have, I'm afraid it is here to stay. All of the magazines talk about the benefits of AI and how you can use it. But nobody is taking into account the fact that if AI is writing books and illustrating books and publishing books why would humans try to compete with that? It takes us a lot longer to come up with an idea and write the story. We have to hire editors when AI just instinctively knows how to write without error.

There was a meme that I saw on social media, it said something like, 'I want AI to learn how to wash my dishes and dust my house so that way I can write books and paint artwork. Not the other way around.' With AI we are going to lose a little bit of ourselves. Our children aren't going to learn how to use their imaginations to come up with stories.

Just this week I saw a video of a new website platform that was 100% AI focused for children. *Teach Tales* It was so simple... A story builder where kids who love to read can create their own adventures. A child could choose their favorite genre, then pick their interests from a whole list of items, or type in their own. They then could choose their setting, their main characters, supporting characters, plot etc. They could create their own characters and bring them to life as AI would automatically create an image or illustration of their character within seconds. And when that is done, the AI would create their story for them. Even the commercial that they put together was done with AI. It was amazing and horrifying.

On one note, I think to myself holy cow my writing career is over. On the other note, I think wow that is so cool. If I would have had access to tech like that growing up, the stories that I could have told and shared... While I love the idea that children can create their own stories quickly and easily, how much of it allows children to actually use their imaginations?

But then I think back to my own writing career. I love reading my own books. Primarily because I know they're exactly what I want to read without wasting my time on something that could be disappointing or contain a subject matter that I would prefer not to read about. If children think the same way, they will write their own stories and not have a need for other authors books. They could even take it a step further and self-publish those stories, written and illustrated with AI.

It's a proven fact that children selling their own books get more sales than adult authors at the same venue. It would be quick. It would be easy. They would make money. But would they actually be developing their skills? Are they truly using their imagination? Or does this take the painstaking effort of writing and turn it into a game? Authors aren't playing. And yet, it almost makes me feel like my craft is being belittled.

AI is coming. I don't know whether it is coming for us, or just our creativity. But with the publishing industry promoting all of the wonderful things that you can do with AI, I have a feeling that even they are going to start utilizing AI instead of human authors. What does that mean for you and your desire to one day have a traditionally published book? That's a good question.

AI Editing

AI can edit your work, but a lot of times it changes it, uses its own words and phrases and can edit your voice right out of the story. It also doesn't catch everything. It doesn't catch repeated sections, name changes, and story flow issues. But it will clean up your sentences and make your story sound great.

AI Illustrations

AI Illustrations are amazing at first glance but the longer you look, the more issues you see. Currently AI still makes tons of mistakes; multiple fingers, weird things in the background, crossed eyes, and more. But give it time, before long it will be replacing artists and illustrators, either that or they will find ways to embrace the technology.

Of course, the old phrase "use it, or lose it" comes to mind. If you embrace AI making illustrations, the art of the past will remain in the past and the legendary artists of today will never become legendary.

AI Writing

You can give AI a topic, or scenario, the genre and the feel you want and it will write you an entire story. At first read, that story will sound amazing. But once you start reading numerous stories written by AI you will find they become repetitive, monotonous, lacking the writer's soul and emotions. They also over-use the em-dash and excel on run-on sentences.

Recording an Audiobook

While AI can read your text and it has come a long way with pronunciation and inflection, it is still boring to listen to and still runs sentences together. A lot of people do not like listening to AI. That being said, at some point down the line, you may not be able to tell the difference. They already have AI voices that sound like famous people.

Fantasy Videos and Book Trailers

AI creates amazing fantasy world graphics and videos. They are short, currently, as extended videos really need more sample content to piece together, but with time, AI will likely be creating our full-length movies. Of course, I don't know what real actors and actresses will do with all of their free time.

AI can now move your eyes to look at the camera after you've read a script on video. They've been able to make an image of you talk for quite a while, so you don't have to. Feeling shy? No problem. Haven't done your make-up, don't worry about it.

Before long, we won't know if we are seeing real people or fake.

AI Reviews

AI reviews are amazingly detailed. When you see one you will be quite impressed, until you start seeing reviews from beta-readers and paid reviewers sound an awful lot like an AI review.

Don't think it matters? How does AI write a review for a book that hasn't been released yet and the beta reader didn't read? Well, AI reads it, of course. Those people, without your knowledge or permission, uploaded your ARC or PDF to AI to read and review so they didn't have to read it. Now AI has added your book to its knowledgebase and will use your creativity when writing stories for non-authors to publish under their name and make money off of.

If all of this sounds great and didn't bother you in the slightest, you are well on your way to joining the society of Wall-e, living out Terminator or The Matrix and experiencing War Games first hand.

But why shouldn't you utilize the technology that everyone else is starting to use? Why shouldn't you get a leg up on the competition? Save money, publish faster, market better? I don't know. Why should you?

Don't Ever Give Up!

One of the greatest things about choosing to self-publish your book rather than going with the traditional publishing route is the fact that you don't have a contract on the life of your book. Most traditional publishers give you about 2 years.

If your book hasn't made the money back that they paid on your advance, which is buying the rights to your story, the story no longer matters to them. They will not pay to print more inventory, and they will remove it from their system.

You will get one last hoorah with your book when they sell it at print cost to places like Usborne Books. And then it's over.

Your book, your character,
your fantasy world, your dream...
is completely over.

But when you self-publish; that book will always be out there. It may not be as prevalent, it may not be as popular, it may not even be your favorite book anymore, but it is still out there.

It is still a feather in your cap. It is still an item in your portfolio. It is still a stepping stone to where you have been and where you are going. It will never go away. You can edit it and make it better and call it a second edition, but the point is, it will always be yours.

With children's books, your readers grow out of your genre pretty darn quickly. Within a couple of years, they won't be reading your book anymore. The good news is, new children will be. Every year you have a brand-new audience born that can read your book.

You could literally figure out what worked, and what didn't work. What shows were good, and what shows were failures. You will have fine-tuned your sales pitch, know exactly what to do, and be able to take your new books out there with all of your old ones and reach brand new audiences in the same location that you were in years before.

That means that every year you publish a new book, you will have more inventory to carry. Yes, that inventory can be heavy, especially if you're doing hardback books! And yes, you will build up muscles hauling all those books to all those shows.

But you know what you're going to accomplish when you do that? Showcasing an astounding display of accomplishments that will wow your future buyers.

So, no matter what, don't ever give up!

As long as you want to keep writing, as long as you choose to keep self-publishing, and as long as you still have the desire and the will to keep going, then do it.

As the world changes around us, as traditional publishers opt for current unpopular fads that may or may not stand up to your specific values, or even the test of time, you will at least be presenting to them, what you feel is important for them to know and read.

In Conclusion

I f you do everything in this book, if you write an amazing story if you hire the best illustrator if you do all of the pre-marketing, post-marketing and advertising. If you win the most prestigious book awards, and if you get hundreds of thousands of reviews, and if you've done everything right, and you're still not able to quit your day job... Welcome to the world of being an author.

I know that sounds disheartening and it shouldn't be that way. But internet algorithms are designed to make it nearly impossible for you to get your information out there. They want you to pay to advertise on their platform. That is how they make money.

Traditional publishers are becoming obsolete with all of the technological advances for self-publishing books. They're holding on to their royal crown as tight as they possibly can and they refuse to let it go. Yet, they still have the money and the power to continue to make the rules and there is not much that a small-time author can do to compete with that. Yet...

Of course, if you do succeed in getting noticed, getting the sales, and making a bold display of your story, you're likely to attract the attention of the traditional publishers, just like JK Rowling did with Harry Potter. Just like William P Young did with the Shack. Just like Christopher Paolini did with Eragon. Traditional publishers will see your success, buy the rights to your story, sell it to Hollywood to be made into a movie and reap the rewards of all of your hard work.

Of course, if that happens, you will have made it. And I would be thrilled if you did it after reading this book. Truly! I am still working towards that goal, myself. I have made many advancements, connections and accolades. I have a book being optioned to film. It is my own goal to meet. And I hope I do.

I hope this book has helped you, enlightened you, and will lead you down the path of success and prosperity. If you liked this book, please consider leaving a review and sharing it with your fellow authors. No matter what, we can all use the help.

God bless your work and God bless you!

About the Author

*K*athleen J. Shields is prolific writer of multiple genres and an award-winning author having won First Place Best Educational Children's Series from the Texas Association of Authors for "The Hamilton Troll Adventures."

She won six book awards and counting for her long-awaited "The First Unibear" rhyming children's story that she wrote when she was only ten years old, multiple awards for "The First Unicorn" and even a win for her Christian fiction trilogy, "The Painting."

While awaiting illustrations, Shields' writes chapter books for her slightly older readers (tweens and general audiences). While still infusing education into each story, Kathleen endeavors to entertain young readers, igniting a desire to read (and maybe even write) that will span a lifetime.

The knowledge and experience she has gained over the decades is generously shared with any who inquire and while her time is limited, she always chooses to provide as much as she can when educating others about their craft.

Shields' runs a website and graphic design company called Kathleen's Graphics. She designs colorful websites, custom logos and advertisements for businesses and authors, she also freelances for printing companies and the like.

She can assist authors with custom book covers, interior formatting and publishing. She can put together book trailer videos, write press releases and so much more. She enjoys being challenged to learn new things and excels when challenged to do so.

Additionally, Kathleen writes an inspirational and educational blog regarding her endeavors as an author as well as a business woman and Christian. Her views are always light-hearted and thought-provoking and are intended to get the reader thinking.

For more information about the author and her books, please visit: **www.KathleensBooks.com** or follow her blog at: **www.KathleenJShields.com**

The Hamilton Troll Adventures

The Hamilton Troll series is educational and inspirational, teaching young children about social skills, animal characteristics, science and how to handle real-life situations.

This multi-award-winning series consists of twelve fully illustrated, rhyming educational stories for bedtime up to 2nd grade. They teach social skills, animal characteristics and even science. Also increase vocabulary by providing definitions to words along with a few fun games inside.

There is also an award-winning Children's Cookbook, a Coloring book and a curriculum workbook to continue the education. Perfect for home school.

Other Books by this Author

Ghost Dogs
As a toddler Jamie develops an amazing gift, the ability to see Ghost Dogs. They look just like our past pets, just transparent.

Turtle Diaries
When a tortoise roams around a turtle sanctuary, fun, education and challenges ensue. He keeps a daily diary of his adventures.

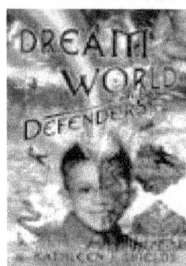

Dream World Defenders
Ryan and his friends enter the dream world where they can do anything they can imagine. Except… Wake up.

ZITS from Outer Space
A Giant Scorpion, a Crab Attack and a Killer Wolf – What do these have in common? The zits on Jared's face!

Ally Cat, A Tale of Survival
Allison Catsworth gets knocked off of a cliff and instead of falling to her death, she transforms into a cat and lands on all four paws!

A Rainbow of Thanks
Kate walks into a rainbow and is transported to various places on the planet as she tries to get back home.

A Rhyme for Everything
A poetry collection of funny, inspirational, musical and simply creative rhyming verses for any occasion.

Dandy Lion, A Legend of Love & Loss Dandy loses a strand of hair each time he helps someone. He sews the seeds of love by doing good deeds.

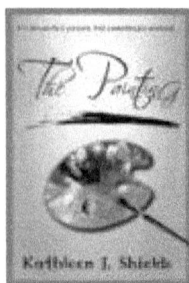

The Painting
Gerald is given a blank canvas, so he paints a world, one that he loves so much – it comes to life!
The First Book of a Trilogy

The Painting 2
Benjamin, Gerald's son, finds a way to be born into the Painting so he can tell the inhabitants about his father, the Painter.

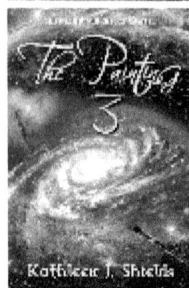

The Painting 3
Nevaeh, the granddaughter of Gerald, imagines herself into the painting. While she's only there in spirit, it's her desire to good that inspires others to act.

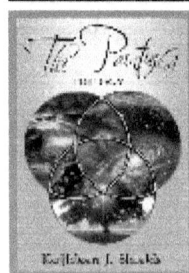

The Painting Trilogy Hard back
The full collection of three stories in a collector's edition hardback book with a beautiful dust jacket.
A must have Collectible!

The First Unibear
A bear rescues a horse that is actually a unicorn. Later, the bear gets a unicorn horn too. A multi award winning inspirational rhyming story.

The First Unicorn
A young horse who helps others, gets bestowed a horn making him the first unicorn. What he can do is simply miraculous.

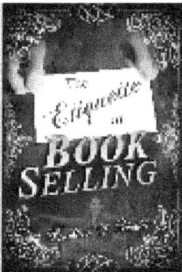

The Etiquette of Book Selling
A how to book encouraging authors to be their best and make a good first impression.

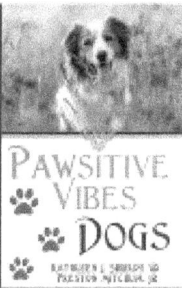

Pawsitive Vibes, Dogs
This fun devotional connects dog emotions and real stories to motivational messages that humans should to take to heart.

Have a Turtle-ific Day
Inspirational Messages for Turtle Lovers explores the life of various species of turtle's through ocean puns, lessons on relaxation, soak up the sun, dream big, slow down, and stay out of trouble.

The Dog Who Cried Woof
Riley takes it upon himself to announce Daddy's return home, but turns it into a game that goes horribly wrong. *Short Story eBook*

Ethan's Reception
FiFi was not happy the day Ethan was brought home from the animal shelter, but Ethan was enthralled! *Short Story eBook*

The Day Hell Froze Over
When the inhabitants of hell begin praying for some cold weather, the devil finds himself in a bind. *Short Story eBook*

And for Young Adults:
The Kaitlyn Jones Trilogy

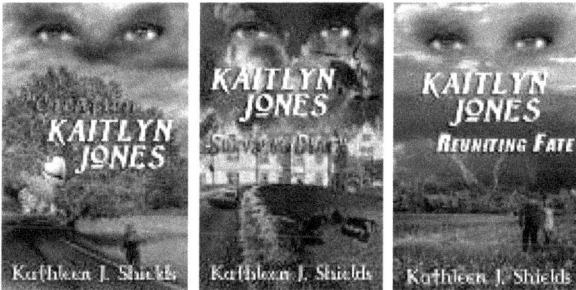

Kaitlyn discovers the gift of precognition, she's able to see things before they happen. She also discovers a telepathic bond with the guy who changed her life and the desire to help others with these gifts. Follow Kaitlyn through High School, her first job as a police officer. When she became a bodyguard, secret service and then secret agent!

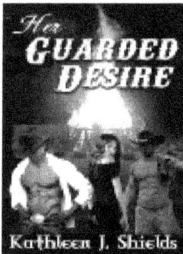

Her Guarded Desire
Kristen must decide between her boyfriend and her bodyguard, when danger reemerges and they are forced on the run.

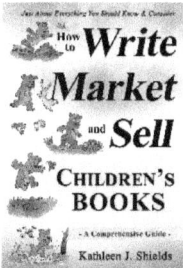

How to Write, Market and Sell Children's Books
This is not a get-rich-quick-scheme. There are no secrets to book publishing. This is an in-depth roadmap to what lies ahead.

141

CRIN GO BRAGH
Publishing

Erin Go Bragh Publishing publishes various genres of books for numerous authors. Their portfolio consists of a 1200-page Vietnamese to English Dictionary, Historical fiction, an award-winning children's educational series, multiple adult novels and memoirs, tween adventure stories, as well as Christian Fiction. Their objective is to promote literacy and education through reading and writing.

www.ErinGoBraghPublishing.com
Canyon Lake, Texas

Interior Illustrations from the following
Erin Go Bragh Publishing Authors' books;
Kathleen J. Shields, Tarif Youssef-Agha

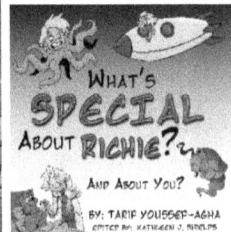

www.ingramcontent.com/pod-product-compliance
Lightning Source LLC
Chambersburg PA
CBHW032036040426
42449CB00007B/913